中國工藝美術商店指南

Shopping in China

Arts, Crafts and the Unusual

Roberta Helmer Stalberg

CHINA BOOKS
& Periodicals, Inc. • San Francisco

Editorial Note

Because of the fluctuation in exchange rates, prices throughout the text have been quoted in Chinese currency rather than converted to values in other currencies. As this book went to press, the Chinese unit of currency, or *yuan*, was valued at 3.7 *yuan* per 1 U.S. dollar, meaning that all prices in this book can be divided by 3.7 to find the equivalent cost in U.S. dollars.

To find the exact rate of exchange before your trip, contact the foreign exchange department of your bank.

Title page calligraphy:	Chu Chan–Kuang
Cover design:	Robbin Henderson
Book design:	Laurie Anderson
Maps:	Eric Duchin and Jennifer Brown
	(Lasha and Tianjin maps by Evelyn Goodman)

Cover painting by Cao Xiuwen
"Celebrating New Year"

Table of Contents

Preface

The last year has brought a host of changes. Some of my favorite stores have moved, closed for renovation, opened after renovation, or closed indefinitely. Free markets continue to be encouraged as an important sector of the Chinese economy, and foreign exchange certificates seem to be here to stay (for this year, at least). Enterprises are aggressively seeking profitable ventures in the present, loosened economic atmosphere, which bodes well for the rise of new shops. The number of stores which accept credit cards has continued to rise, as has the range of cards accepted. All of these factors have worked to make shopping opportunities in China more diverse. They also make a book like *Shopping in China* more important than ever.

I have included only those sources I believe are of high standard and special interest for their merchandising and services. Thankfully, you can still find many sources for extraordinary crafts in China. And this guide will help you do it.

In this edition I have added shopping information on two new cities: Lhasa and Tianjin. I have added the former city with a certain amount of trepidation due to the unsettled state of affairs in Lhasa at the end of 1987. All evidence appears to indicate, however, that group tours will not be halted and that foreigners will continue to be able to visit this unique city.

As a final note, I am always happy to receive letters from travelers who have found conditions at stores to be other than indicated in this book. Management changes, service may decline, and merchandise may deteriorate. I worry in particular about the troubling tendency to manufacture "souvenir" commodities at the expense of authentic, traditional local crafts. Informed, inquiring shoppers are the best antidote to this worldwide trend, and I hope that *Shopping in China* will encourage travelers to seek out the best that China has to offer.

Roberta Helmer Stalberg, New York, New York
December, 1987

Acknowledgments

During the research for this book, a number of people have revisited stores to confirm, expand, or update information. My thanks go to the following for their enthusiasm and assistance: Christopher Stalberg, Anita Christy, George Chu, Janie Shen, Li-wen Zhang, Laurance Hoo, Beate Gordon, Yu Shilian, Diane Maas, Louisa Schein, Shen Fengming, Roberta White, and Lorna McCarr. I want to thank Sandy Keef for the use of a computer when mine was lost in moving, and Li-mei and Li-ying Chen for all their help. Warm thanks also go to Mr. Chu Chen-Kuang for his fine calligraphy on the title page.

The staff at China Books and Periodicals has provided numerous useful suggestions during the writing of this guide. To Nancy Ippolito and Foster Stockwell, my editor, I am particularly indebted for valuable comments and recommendations.

Chronology of Chinese Dynasties

Xia (Hsia) Dynasty   ca. 21st–16th centuries BC

Shang (Yin) Dynasty   ca. 16th century–1066 BC

Zhou (Chou) Dynasty   ca. 1066–256 BC
    Western Zhou (Chou) / ca. 1066–77 BC
    Eastern Zhou (Chou) / 770–256 BC
    Spring and Autumn Period / 772–481 BC
    Warring States Period / 403–221 BC

Qin (Ch'in) Dynasty   221–206 BC

Han Dynasty   206 BC–AD 220
    Western Han / 206 BC–AD 23
    Eastern Han / 25–220

Three Kingdoms Period*   220–316
    State of Wei / 220–65
    State of Shu / 221–63
    State of Wu / 222–80

Western Jin (Tsin) Dynasty   265–316

Eastern Jin (Tsin) Dynasty and Sixteen States   317–439
    Eastern Jin (Tsin) / 317–420
    Sixteen States / 304–439

*The Three Kingdoms Period, the Western Jin Dynasty, and the Eastern Jin Dynasty and Sixteen States are also known as the Six Dynasties.

Southern and Northern Dynasties   386–581

Southern Dynasties
Song (Sung) / 420–79
Qi (Ch'i) / 429–502
Liang / 502–57
Chen (Ch'en) / 557–89
Northern Dynasties)
Northern Wei / 386–534
Eastern Wei / 534–50
Northern Qi (Ch'i) / 550–77
Western Wei / 535–57
Northern Zhou (Chou) / 557–81

Sui Dynasty   581–618

Tang (T'ang) Dynasty   618–907

Five Dynasties and Ten Kingdoms Period   907–79
Later Liang / 907–23
Later Tang (T'ang) / 923–36
Later Jin (Tsin) / 936–46
Later Han / 947–50
Later Zhou (Chou) / 951–60
Ten Kingdoms / 902–79

Song (Sung) Dynasty   960–1279
Northern Song (Sung) / 960–1127
Southern Song (Sung) / 1127–1279

Liao (Kitan) Dynasty   907–1125

Western Xia (Hsia) Dynasty   1032–1227

Jin (Nurchen) Dynasty   1115–1234

Yuan (Mongol) Dynasty   1279–1368

Ming Dynasty   1368–1644

Qing (Manchu) Dynasty   1644–1911

Republic of China   1912–1949

People's Republic of China   Established 1949

中国旅行略图

CHINA

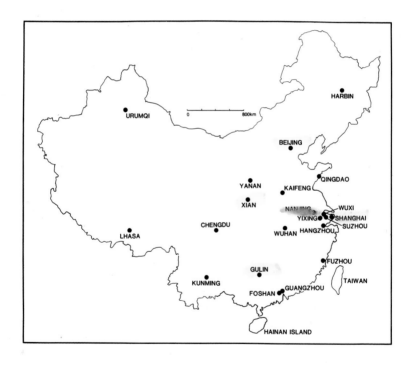

URUMQI

0   800km

HARBIN

BEIJING

QINGDAO

YANAN   KAIFENG

XIAN   NANJING   WUXI

CHENGDU   YIXING   SHANGHAI
                                    SUZHOU
LHASA   WUHAN   HANGZHOU

                              FUZHOU

GULIN   TAIWAN

KUNMING

          FOSHAN GUANGZHOU

          HAINAN ISLAND

Overview

Shopping in China—the very words evoke images of exotic bazaars replete with curious treasures, from the graceful wares of a curbside dough sculptor to the shimmering silks of an elaborate urban emporium. Present day Marco Polos can still feel the excitement of seeing objects made much as they have been for centuries. Indeed, shopping in China is an experience that can link the present to China's long artistic heritage.

China is presently undergoing a tremendous burst of economic growth and change. This expansion has brought new convenience and opportunities for the 10 million overseas tourists who visit China every year. There are now over 30 duty–free shops in China, and seven international credit cards are accepted in major cities. Visitors may cash traveler's checks issued by over 40 international banks, while the number of cities and counties open to tourism has risen to 257.

The new consumer–oriented mood is conspicuous in all city department stores, which today carry much more than the bare essentials of a few years ago. A visit to a major city department store is a must, not only because this allows you to compare prices with those in other outlets, but because it gives some feeling for everyday Chinese life.

How this Book Came About

I have visited China many times since 1980, sometimes doing cultural research and sometimes leading groups of tourists on special–interest tours. Frequently these visits involved side trips to craft centers, factory outlets, and free markets where I was called upon to translate craft terms from Chinese to English. On these excursions it also fell to me to explain the meanings of symbols and to help negotiate final selections and prices. These experiences may have left me feeling harassed, but they never left me bored.

I firmly believe that shopping can be a cultural experience which provides fascinating glimpses into Chinese life—from sophisticated Beijing couples painstakingly selecting porcelains on Wangfujing Street to old farming women hawking their bold, hand embroidered baby hats at a Xian free market.

In my travels I have always searched for unique, high–quality stores. In the following pages I am happy to suggest what I consider the best store for painting brushes, inkstones, and other art supplies, the best market for woven baskets, and the prime source for old opera costumes.

Shops dealing in crafts, antiques, and folk art are mushrooming everywhere in China, with new ones opening each day.

A guide such as this is essential, thus, for anyone hoping to navigate through the vast array of retail outlets to find distinctive craft items among the wide variety available. In writing the book, I have always tried to keep you—the reader and traveler—in mind. I have held your needs first and foremost, doing the tedious and time–consuming research so that you can make the most of your time in China. I have tried to anticipate your questions, as if you were traveling with me, and I have written the store descriptions accordingly. I hope the book's contents will add to the pleasure and success of your trip.

How to Get the Most out of this Book

The 14 cities selected for inclusion in this book are all popular stops on current group itineraries and all of them are important for some type of craft production. The retail outlets recommended in each city include arts and crafts stores, crafts research institutes, factory retail outlets, exhibition halls, museum stores, archeological sites, and free markets. I have even included several private artists' studios and plan to increase this category of entry in future editions.

The size, layout, and services provided by each outlet vary according to the type, but each source has been carefully selected for its uniqueness, high standards, or some other special quality.

In order to get the most from your limited time in China, I suggest you begin by reading as much as possible about the major kinds of Chinese crafts, the way they are made, the meaning of key symbols, and what regions specialize in what crafts. If you are still choosing an itinerary, this book will help you focus on which cities are the best sources for specific crafts. If your itinerary is already set, on the other hand, it is a simple matter to check the sources listed under each city to find those that interest you most.

Arranged by city, each section includes a map showing the location of the retail outlets described, along with a brief introduction to the cultural history of the city, information about traditional local crafts, and descriptions of the major shopping areas. Store entries include the address, telephone number, manager's name (where available), business hours, forms of payment, and whether the salespeople speak English. Remember that many Chinese businesses close for lunch, especially during the summer, from around noon until 1 or even 2 p.m. It is always wise to telephone ahead before planning a visit during these hours.

For visitors interested in a particular type of art, I have included a special section that explains key terms and how various crafts are made. This section also clarifies regional differences in crafts, important symbols and their meanings, and signs of good craftsmanship. Here, for example, you can find the meaning of "celadon" or read exactly how cloisonne is made.

Chinese characters haved been provided for all store names and addresses, which allow visitors to point to the Chinese terms when asking for help. Armed with this information and the locations provided by the city maps, you should be able to find any store listed in this book. Once you reach the store, you can use the glossary to ask for the crafts you want. All you have to do is point to the characters.

At the time of your visit, merchandise and prices may not necessarily be the same as those listed in this book. These are the areas of fastest change in China today and no guidebook can immediately reflect these changes. Acceptable methods of payment may change also, with the trend being for more stores to accept non–cash forms of payment such as traveler's checks and credit cards. Free markets can also be expected to grow in number. The Chinese government has announced that it plans to open some 30,000 free markets all over the country in order to create a national system of free markets by 1990. Although most of these will specialize in food and farm products, visitors can expect to find local crafts, second–hand goods, and furniture.

As a final note, I should point out that this guide is not an all–inclusive, indiscriminate index. I have included only those sources which I believe are of high standards and special interest for distinctive merchandise and services. I have not included ordinary shops, such as hotel gift counters or friendship stores, unless they fulfill these criteria and have unusual offerings.

My selections are necessarily somewhat subjective, based on my preference for the unique and the traditional, the fine piece fashioned with loving attention to detail. This book also reflects my bias against the pedestrian souvenir commodities that appear to be flooding the world.

I am glad to say that you can still find many sources for extraordinary crafts in China. This guide will help you do it.

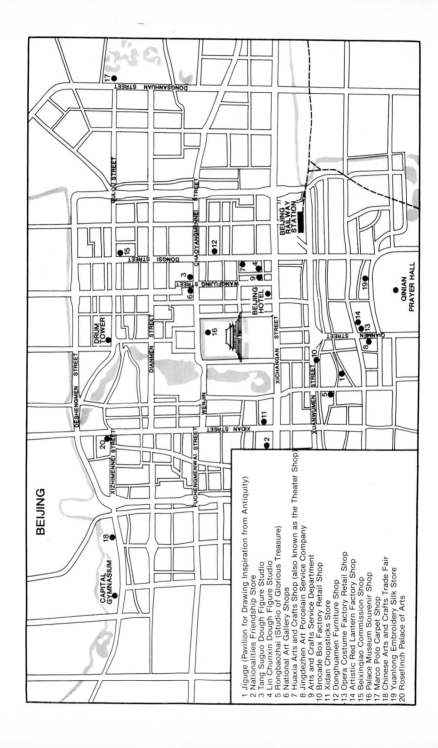

BEIJING

1 Jiguge (Pavilion for Drawing Inspiration from Antiquity)
2 Nationalities Friendship Store
3 Tang Suguo Dough Figure Studio
4 Lin Chunxin Dough Figure Studio
5 Rongbaozhai (Studio of Glorious Treasure)
6 National Art Gallery Shops
7 Huaxia Arts and Crafts Shop (also known as the Theater Shop)
8 Jingdezhen Art Porcelain Service Company
9 Arts and Crafts Service Department
10 Brocade Box Factory Retail Shop
11 Xidan Chopsticks Store
12 Donghuamen Furniture Shop
13 Opera Costume Factory Retail Shop
14 Artistic Red Lantern Factory Shop
15 Beixinqiao Commission Shop
16 Palace Museum Souvenir Shop
17 Marco Polo Carpet Shop
18 Chinese Arts and Crafts Trade Fair
19 Yuanlong Embroidery Silk Store
20 Rosefinch Palace of Arts

Beijing

From the glinting orange–glazed tiles and roof guardians of the Summer Palace to the formal white marble sculpture of the Forbidden City, Beijing is a vast museum housing some of the finest examples of China's crafts traditions. It is a city conscious of its imperial past, a city which has long had a reputation for excellence in creating superb objects from the finest materials.

Beijing has a recorded history of 3,000 years, during which its location on the edge of the North China Plain has given it a continuing strategic importance in trade. For almost 1,000 years a capital under various dynasties, the city survived while dynasties rose and fell around it. When Kublai Khan established the Yuan Dynasty in the 13th century, he made his grand new capital here, collecting craftsmen conscripted from throughout the vast Mongol territories to provide luxuries for his palaces. At this time the Mongol empire stretched throughout East Asia from Korea and Manchuria in the north to North Vietnam in the south, through Central Asia, Persia, and Russia. Persians, Central Asians, Armenians and even Europeans brought their special skills at the working of gold and silver and brightly colored enamels to this cosmopolitan center.

The famous traveler Marco Polo described his amazement at the magnificence of Khan–balik, "the city of the Khan," when he visited the Mongol capitol at the end of the 13th century.

> I assure you that the streets are so broad and straight that from the top of the wall above one gate you can see along the whole length of the road to the gate opposite. The city is full of fine man-

sions, inns, and dwelling–houses. All the way down the sides of every main street there are booths and shops of every sort. All the building sites throughout the city are square and measured by the rule; and on every site stand large and spacious mansions with ample courtyards and gardens. These sites are allotted to heads of households, so that one belongs to such–and–such a person, representing such–and–such a family, the next to a representative of another family, and so all the way along. Every site or block is surrounded by good public roads; and in this way the whole interior of the city is laid out in squares like a chess–board with such masterly precision that no description can do justice to it.

In this city there is such a multitude of houses and of people, both within the walls and without, that no one could count their number. Actually there are more people outside the walls in the suburbs than in the city itself. There is a suburb outside every gate, such that each one touches the neighbouring suburbs on either side. They extend in length for three or four miles. And in every suburb or ward, at about a mile's distance from the city, there are many fine hostels which provide lodging for merchants coming from different parts: a particular hostel is assigned to every nation, as we might say one for the Lombards, another for the Germans, another for the French. Merchants and others come here on business in great numbers, both because it is the Khan's residence and because it affords a profitable market...

You may take it for a fact that more precious and costly wares are imported into Khan–balik than into any other city in the world. Let me give you particulars. All the treasures that come from India—precious stones, pearls, and other rarities—are brought here. So too are the choicest and costliest products of Cathay itself and every other province. This is on account of the Great Khan himself, who lives here, and of the lords and ladies and the enormous multitude of hotel–keepers and other residents and of visitors who attend the courts held here by the Khan. That is why the volume and value of the imports and of the internal trade exceed those of any other city in the world. It is a fact that every day more than 1,000 cart–loads of silk enter the city; for much cloth of gold and silk is woven here. Furthermore, Khan–balik is surrounded by more than 200 other cities, near and far, from which traders come to it to sell and buy. So it is not surprising that it is the centre of such traffic as I have described.(Ronald Latham, trans., *The Travels of Marco Polo*, New York: Penguin Books, 1958, pp. 128–30.)

The Mongol rule was short–lived, however, and Chinese control was restored in 1368 with the establishment of the Ming Dynasty. It was the third Ming emperor, Yong–le, who brought Beijing into the limelight once again as the Chinese capital. When he chose to move his court north from Nanjing in the early 15th century, he ordered a vast force of thousands of craftsmen to accompany him to undertake the immense job of totally reconstructing the Imperial Palace as well as providing every sort of luxurious craft in its decoration.

Some argue that Beijing craftsmen reached their heights during the following Qing Dynasty, when the Kang–xi emperor established 27 imperial workshops within the palace grounds to create costly crafts of glass, bronze, gold, enamel, cloisonné, lacquer, jade, and ivory for the use of the court. With their establishment in 1680, the most skilled craftsmen were brought here to work. The Qian–long emperor, who ruled from 1736–1795, was especially zealous in his patronage of luxurious crafts, and the resulting output was prodigious and marked by a polished virtuosity. A great lover of jade, Qian–long ordered that the finest jade from the Western frontiers be shipped directly to these imperial workshops for their exclusive use, a directive which was largely circumvented by enterprising merchants who diverted much of the jade for sale to private shops.

By the 20th century China's economic and political instability had largely destroyed the demand for luxury crafts. Beijing's skilled craftsmen needed the patronage of the court or of wealthy merchants to survive because their techniques were time–consuming and their materials costly. Without this support they were reduced to making trinkets such as jewelry, amulets, chopsticks, and mah–jong pieces—often sold as curios to foreigners—just in order to eke out a subsistence living. Under these circumstances, quality declined and patterns dwindled. By one estimate, for example, there were only about 100 jade carvers left in Beijing by 1950.

With the founding of the People's Republic in 1949, Beijing's crafts workshops began to grow busy again, the old skills still evident. Today visitors to the city's cloisonné, jade, ivory, carpet, and lacquer factories will see continuing traditions being passed down to the new generation of artisans. While the city continues to excel in these costly crafts, the folk crafts have not been forgotten. A 61–year–old retired carpenter and his family have made a household workshop to construct colorfully painted silk kites of phoenixes, eagles, and even a tiny butterfly. Along the narrow lanes or *hutongs*, skilled craft workers continue to fashion dough figures and painted leather shadow figures by hand, just as has been done for generations.

What to Look For

Visitors to Beijing are fortunate in being able to select from not only local craft specialties but wares from all over the country. A number of the city's stores send representatives throughout China to purchase fine quality items. Thus you may find the greatest variety and highest quality of pieces from which to choose. In addition, some objects have been commissioned by special order and cannot be found for sale even in the areas where they were made. With a little preparation and know how, you will be able to get beyond the standard souvenirs which most visitors bring home.

Beijing excels in the following crafts: carved cinnabar lacquer, jade and ivory carving, cloisonné, silver and gold filigree, carpets, water color wood–block prints, interior painted snuff bottles, and embroidered Beijing opera costumes. In addition to the expensive local specialties, knowledgeable visitors will find folk crafts such as kites, small figures made of dough and silk, palace–style lanterns, and shadow figures.

Where to Look

The visitor to Beijing will find much of the city's history preserved in the alleys and lanes known as *hutongs* (a word of Mongolian origin) which checker the city. There are over 4,000 such lanes, of which the narrowest is only 28 inches across. The names of many of these lanes reflect the old location of busy markets which specialized in one type of merchandise, such as Dengshikou (Lantern Market Crossroad), Zhushikou (Pearl Market Crossroad), Zhubaoshi (Jewelry Market), Huashi (Flower Market), Gangwashi (Pottery Market), as well as similarly named streets of markets for pigs, sheep, horses, rice, fish, etc. Although the markets are gone, their memory is preserved in Beijing's old street names.

Today there are three major shopping districts in the city: Wangfujing, Liulichang, and Qianmen.

Wangfujing Street runs north and south, crossing Changan Avenue just east of the Beijing Hotel. Its name in Chinese, "Well of the Princes' Mansions," refers to a well located here near the mansions of ten Ming Dynasty hereditary princes. The well is thought to have existed just south of the large Beijing Department Store at No. 255. In imperial days it was strictly forbidden to excavate wells near the imperial palace for fear of upsetting the *feng–shui*, or balance of natural forces, of the imperial palace. If these forces were disturbed, it was believed that the dynasty could be toppled.

Before 1949, foreigners called this Morrison Street, in recognition of the dynamic and sometimes ruthless London Times correspondent who lived on the west side of the street at No. 98. With the proximity of the foreign community in the former Legation Quarter directly south of Wangfujing, the area became a thriving shopping center which carried expensive goods for foreign tastes.

Today this street contains over 100 shops and is one of the busiest in all Beijing. Bustling and crowded all the time, on holidays it is nearly impassable.

Liulichang Street runs east and west, intersecting South Xinhua Road south of the Peace Gate (Hepingmen). The street name, "Glazed Tile Factory," is derived from the glazed tile works which were located in this area as early as the 13th century. When the extensive construction of the Imperial Palace began under the Ming Dynasty, in the 14th century, a complex of special kilns for the production of glazed tiles and bricks was established here. In addition to golden roof tiles for the Imperial Palace, the kilns also produced clay whistles and toys.

During the Ming and Qing Dynasties the area became a market for curio and antique dealers and a center for shops selling paintings, calligraphy, artists' supplies, and old books. By the 18th century the street had over 30 bookshops where scholars flocked from all over China to buy, browse, and meet fellow scholars.

> Bespectacled old gentlemen (who may have one or more degrees of Imperial Examinations to their credit) would look

around here, examining the shelves of books and some voluminous works boxed in camphorwood chests for protection against moths. Silent and careful, they seem to be entirely absorbed in their hunt for rare books, checking over with their own collections. These are the regular book–worms and "oracles on points of learning"...Some of these people are known to be rapid readers and it is said that while they bargain with the booksellers about the prices, they would, by what seems to be a mere fingering of the pages, memorize all that is worth while in some lesser volumes and when this is done they would have no more need to buy the books except for the purpose of adding them to their collections. (H.Y. Lowe, *The Adventures of Wu*, Princeton: Princeton University Press, 1983, pp. 177–8.)

During the lunar New Year Liulichang became one huge bazaar crammed with stalls and booths selling every sort of toy and lantern, as well as local specialties such as sweet black bean soup or sour plum tea.

The shops of Liulichang have recently been completely restored in traditional style, and most are now open for business once again.

Qianmen, or the Front Gate, was the largest of three gates which opened between the old Northern or Tartar City and the Chinese City to the south. The cities were so named because, during the Qing Dynasty, the Manchus lived in the north and restricted all ethnic Chinese to the southern walled city. A Qing law prohibited "uproarious noises" in the northern city near the Imperial Palace, and as a result numerous shops and entertainments sprang up in the crowded lanes south of the gate. Of all the city gates, this one alone was reopened each night shortly after midnight so that officials who had been spending the evening at various entertainment establishments south of the gate could return in time for the early morning audience with the emperor.

One of the most interesting streets of the Qianmen district is Dashanlan, ("the great wicker barrier") Street. Since the 14th century such barriers were put in place to close off streets after curfew to insure public order at night. Later the practice died out, but the name still reflects this old custom. Dashanlan, in the past known to foreign residents as Silk Street, was famous for its large silk shops and stores which sold imported merchandise. (Note that the street is sometimes spelled Dazhalan or Dazhanlan, reflecting the local Beijing pronunciation, which is close to "Dazhalar.")

Today the narrow street houses almost 40 establishments, some of the city's oldest in continual existence. The street is always crowded, serving 100,000 customers on an average day and twice that on holidays.

Note to those shopping for antiques: Be aware that items over 100 years old are required to carry a red or brown wax seal attesting to the fact that they may be taken out of China. (These seals do not necessarily indicate that an item is antique, as some newer objects as well as high-quality reproductions may also be so marked.) If you buy old objects without such seals—at a free market, for example—it is a good idea to have them approved for export and marked at the Beijing Art Objects Clearance Office located in the compound behind the Friendship Store on Jianguomenwai Street. The service is provided Monday through Friday from 2–5 p.m.

Highly Recommended Stores ★ ★

1. Jiguge ★ ★
(Pavilion for Drawing Inspiration from Antiquity)
136 East Liulichang Street
Telephone: 335698; 334531, ext.250

汲古阁
琉璃厂东于136 号

Manager: Fan Shuzeng
Public Relations Manager: Walter V.C. Cao (Cao Weiqing)

Hours: 9–6

Accepts traveler's checks and all major credit cards (such as American Express, Diner's Club, Visa, and Master Charge)

Can arrange for items to be shipped overseas
Has English–speaking staff

Recommended Crafts

- reproduction of an unglazed Han Dynasty ceramic figurine of an exuberant storyteller beating a drum to accompany his recitation

- reproduction of an 18th century nine–peach vase (350 *yuan*)
- green glazed Han Dynasty figurines
- intricate bronze Warring States Period vessel with gold inlay (8,000 *yuan*)
- life size reproduction of a Qin warrior (5,000 *yuan*)
- colorful rubbings of ancient stone carvings (2–20 *yuan*)

This fascinating shop is highly recommended for any visitor to Beijing. Jiguge is a key store in Beijing's major art and antiquities area known as Liulichang. Along with the 52 other shops on this old street, Jiguge has been undergoing a top–to–bottom refurbishing, which was completed late in 1985. Now the shop is restored in traditional style with decorative wood lattice work, tile roof, third story balustrade, and colorful gold details. Since the 18th century this street has been famous for its fine paintings, books, antiques, and crafts, and Jiguge continues this heritage by specializing in museum–quality reproductions of ceramics and bronzes from almost every historical period.

The store was established 30 years ago when about 30 Liulichang curio shops were collectivized to sell their wares jointly. Later the sale of fine quality reproductions replaced the sale of antiques. Today 80% of the store's reproductions are made from objects in the collection of the Palace Museum, often by special commission. The store has its own workshop where fine old pieces are brought for study and reproduction. It is possible to visit the workshop by special arrangement if you have a concrete reason for such a request, but arrangements should be scheduled well in advance of your trip.

A visit to Jiguge is a distinctive experience. Before you turn down Liulichang Street, you may see street peddlars selling traditional Beijing delicacies, such as fried cakes with chestnut paste, sweet potatoes baked open air, crullers, and mashed pea cakes. You may even see an old man with trained dogs and monkeys performing tricks. As you enter Jiguge, the atmosphere will change, however, and you will feel as if you have entered an intimate museum. On the first floor are smaller ceramic figurines, Qing–style embroideries, silver and gold filigree objects, rubbings, and seals. The store's most impressive pieces are found on the second floor, which one enters through a doorway flanked by group of silent terra cotta warriors reproduced from the figures at the tomb of the Qin emperor outside Xian.

The shopper can find both quality and quantity here, from elegant reproductions of Han ceramic figurines selling for 20 *yuan*, to a complete bronze chariot with terra cotta charioteer and three horses, reproduced from the extraordinary set which was recently discovered at the Qin emperor's tomb. Jiguge reproduced three of these chariots (which are the largest bronze reproductions in China) by special commission, and sold one set to a Paris museum. Another set is currently on display in the store. The last set can be yours for only 3,000,000 *yuan* (about $800,000, at current exchange rates). The store also accepts large orders from all over the world, reproducing rubbings of paintings and calligraphy from the Palace Museum in lots of 60–100,000 at a time for Japanese buyers.

But the buyer who shops on a smaller scale is also very welcome here. As you wander through the rooms of Jiguge, you may feel the same hushed awe that you have during a visit to a fine museum. At every turn it is obvious that the reproductions here have been lovingly fashioned by craftsmen with a strong sense of China's past. The store's staff, of whom quite a few speak good English, also take great pride in their wares and are quite knowledgeable about the history of the pieces (an awareness not seen in many stores in China, unfortunately).

If you are especially lucky, you may be able to go through the store escorted by Walter V. C. Cao, the store's knowledgeable and informative public relations director. In his gentle, cultured manner, Mr. Cao will conduct you on a tour of some of the finest art objects of China's long history, imparting fascinating details of craft tradition and technique as well as some wonderful anecdotes about the difficulty of meeting the sometimes insatiable demands of international art buyers. Mr. Cao and the staff can also provide a fact–filled background for any piece available in the store. If you travel with a group, you might also call ahead and arrange for a briefing about the store, which will give some useful insights.

If you plan to place a large order for the store's crafts, you may end up negotiating with Mr. Fan, the store manager. Here, as in the rest of China, do not be misled by the manager's casual dress and attitude. He has negotiated million–dollar deals with major museums and dealers all over the world. He knows precisely the value of his merchandise and he, like the rest of the staff, is proud of the store's reputation for quality work.

2. Nationalities Friendship Store ★ ★

Fuchengmennei Avenue, at the Nationalities Cultural Palace,
main building, 2nd floor
Telephone: 662923; 653231, ext.423

民族友谊商店
复兴门内大于

Manager: Zhu Bin
Staff member: Liu Wei

Hours: 8–5, closed Monday. The hours are irregular in the
summer, when the shop is sometimes closed in the morning.

Accepts traveler's checks but no credit cards

No English–speaking staff

Recommended Crafts

- colorful Zhuang tapestries from Guangxi (80–150 *yuan*)
- appliquéd Mongolian leather boots (80 *yuan*)
- long brocade Mongolian robes (60–150 *yuan*)
- Tang san–cai glazed ceramic horse (4 *yuan*)

The Nationalities Friendship Store is a "must see" for anyone interested in Chinese folk art or minority costumes. The shop is housed on the second floor in the main building of the imposing Nationalities Cultural Palace, which was built in 1959 to promote the art and culture of China's minorities. Along with a library and theater, the complex contains a museum with 18 halls displaying the distinctive costumes, crafts, ornaments, musical instruments, and lifestyles of China's 55 national minority peoples.

Although these people make up only 6% of the country's total population, they occupy more than 50% of the country's total terrain, most of it in strategic border areas. This gives them an importance beyond that of numbers alone. The visitor who cannot travel to the Mongolian steppes, the Taklamakan Desert, or the highlands of Tibet will find something of the culture of these regions' natives represented in the halls at the Nationalities Cultural Palace.

The Nationalities Friendship Store's floor space is not large, but within its walls are concentrated unique examples of embroidery, weaving, jewelry, and leatherwork from many far flung regions of China. The shop was opened in 1979 as an outlet for the sale of minority goods to Chinese and foreigners, and its crafts are selected from retail stores throughout China's minority areas. This is probably the only place in China where under one roof a visitor can purchase a Mongolian yurt (only 1,300 *yuan*, but the price is negotiable), Tibetan hiking boots, Miao silver jewelry, or colorful Zhuang minority tapestries from the southeast province of Guangxi.

Mongolian wares always seem to be unusually well represented here, with hand tooled and colorfully appliquéd Mongolian leather boots (a good buy at 80 *yuan* if you can find your size), dazzling silk brocade Mongolian robes with side closing for 60 to 150 *yuan*, and Mongolian copper or bronze hot pots at 80 *yuan*. Rainbow colored, woven Tibetan sashes are very inexpensive at 12 *yuan*, or you may choose an exquisitely woven Yi minority sarong of red and green against a black ground (120 *yuan*).

This is the only store of its type in China. (We were told that the management tried to establish another one in Shanghai, but the venture failed.) The store aims to represent as many nationalities as possible in its merchandise, but items may vary markedly depending upon local availability.

The shop has become quite a busy place these days, as new economic policies are providing the Chinese with more disposable income. Han ethnic Chinese as well as minority peoples shop in the store, the latter often students or visitors to the capitol. On one of our visits we rubbed elbows with Korean women from China's northeast Liaoning Province choosing embroidered ribbons for their graceful traditional gowns, and Tibetans buying green felt hats and silver jewelry. In addition to dress items, you can find "Persian–style" carpets from the northwest region of Xinjiang, cooking utensils, and all types of batik bags and fabric.

Reflecting the customs of many of China's minorities who wear elaborate necklaces, earrings, and headdresses, the shop sells a wide variety of silver and gold jewelry, and even carries jewelry tools and individual pieces to make your own finished items.

On a recent visit, however, one of the best buys we found at the store was a colorful Tang–Dynasty–style ceramic horse with dripping glaze known as *Tang sancai*. It sold here for only four *yuan*, much cheaper than could be found elsewhere, even at the factory in Luoyang. Be careful to check for defects such as cracks or chipping, however. As in most of China, quality control is accomplished at the time of sale, when it is considered the buyer's responsibility to check for flaws before the sale is completed.

Another note of caution in an otherwise high recommendation is that the objects in the shop are identified solely in Chinese (and quite sparsely at that). Salespeople speak virtually no English and are not well informed about the source or use of the objects sold. If you do not have a translator, you may want to ask a Chinese friend to accompany you on your visit. Finally, the purist may discern some disturbing modern touches in traditional craft techniques or motifs, such as the village name which is now embroidered on Sani bags sold as souvenirs of the Stone Forest in Yunnan Province.

In spite of these caveats, the discerning visitor will find much to delight in here. If you cannot visit the minority areas, you will find the Nationalities Friendship Store a memorable addition to your China trip.

3. Dough Figure Studio of Tang Suguo ★ ★
Located at the Central Academy of Fine Art
5 Xiaowei Hutong, 10th floor
Beijing's East City District
Telephone: 554731, ext.235

汤夙国先生
东城区校尉胡同 10 楼 5 号

No set hours; must call first to arrange for appointment

Recommended Crafts

Although all his sculptures are impressive, some of my favorites are:
- a brooding Othello
- a dazzling sculpture of opera figure Bai Qi caught in a dramatic pose
- Buddhist figure known as "Long–eyebrowed Arhat"
- world–weary old monk with young novice attendant

- amazing dough landscapes sculpted within a half–walnut shell, an art invented by Tang Zibo

The craft of dough figurine sculpture has been passed down by Chinese folk artists for centuries. It is said that dough was first used over 2,000 years ago to make effigies of malevolent spirits, which were then destroyed to control their power. Later the craft was popularized at street markets and seasonal festivals where itinerant artisans sold their inexpensive colored miniatures to a crowd of eager children for a few cents apiece. But in the late 19th century a scholar named Tang Zibo (1882–1971) brought a keen eye and new vigor to this traditional craft by studying every facet of a character and then capturing the essence of the person within a few deft movements. Today Tang Zibo's son, Tang Suguo, maintains the high standards set by his father, creating one–of–a–kind artistic pieces in his studio at the Central Academy of Fine Arts, where he is an associate professor. Energetic and somewhat flamboyant for a Chinese, Tang is faithful to the tradition of dough sculpture but has expanded the repertoire to include subjects such as Othello, Einstein, and Seiji Ozawa. In 4 or 5 inches he brings to life a character's whole personality and creates a complete world in microcosm. For those who are sincerely interested in or are serious collectors of folk art and sculpture, a visit to Tang Suguo's studio is an experience not to be forgotten.

Tang Zibo began to evolve his distinctive style of fine dough sculpture in 1895, devising his own method of mixing and coloring the dough. Forgoing the traditional method of using bamboo splints and strings to hold the miniatures in shape, the artist devised a new way of support. He developed a blend of wheat and rice flour with oil and preservatives, which he steamed so that the figures would never crack, fade, or lose their shape. Silk fabric, sequins, and gold or silver clothed the figures in traditional costumes, while silk floss created the hair. Tang's motto was "go from the internal to reach the outward appearance and move from externals to attain the inner essence, so that the dough figures seem to be born of the spirit of the dough itself."

Today 50–year old Tang Suguo draws upon elements of classical Chinese painting and traditional folk arts to create his vivid and lively figures. His training in literature, calligraphy and painting gives a greater refinement to his pieces. In his studio, of which one wall is lined with the vivid and startling detailed examples of his art, Tang will discourse enthusiastically upon this fascinating craft, speaking with some

English. On another wall hangs an imposing portrait of his father in dignified mandarin robes and long beard. Lively and spry, his son bears little resemblance to the man in the portrait. With long prematurely gray hair and a somewhat avant garde air, Tang Suguo has developed his own distinctive sculpting style.

Before he begins a sculpture, Tang says, he often must paint 100 pictures to achieve the exact facial expression which he is looking for. Only then does he throw them all away and sit down to sculpt. After kneading bits of colorful dough and pressing the material into fine threads, Tang wields an ox–horn stick to fashion the craggy face of a world–weary old Buddhist monk. In another work he captures the spirit of Zhong Kui, the demon chaser, whose fiercely ugly face was thought to repel demons at one glance. Tang's figures are easy to understand but never commonplace. It is a measure of respect that he and his father are known in China as the "Doughmen Tang."

Although Tang Suguo is kept busy with his teaching, research and sculpture, he is happy to receive collectors or those with a serious appreciation for Chinese folk art. In keeping with Tang's reputation, his figures do not come cheap—you should be prepared to spend upward of 200 *yuan* for his lower–priced pieces and much more for his one–of–a–kind "artistic pieces." Because of the wealth of background information which he can provide and the chance to see his impressive collection of dough sculptures, a visit to the studio of Tang Suguo will be a memorable experience.

Note: Mr. Tang has kindly extended a welcome to readers of this book, but we feel it is our responsibility to ask that only those with a specialized interest in the subject contact the artist, because he is a busy man with many demands on his time.

Other Beijing Dough Sculptors

Although Tang Suguo has taken a decidedly scholarly approach to his art, there are many other people with more modest goals and skills who make less recherche dough figures. If you go into almost any Beijing neighborhood and ask for a dough sculptor you probably will be able to find one. We found a young man, Lin Chunxin, hard at work in his home studio several lanes behind the Beijing Arts and Crafts Store on Wang-fujing Street.

Lin developed his skills through training at the Children's Palace in Beijing. Every day he works at his desk, kneading dough and modeling tiny figures beneath a single fluorescent desk lamp into the small hours of the morning. Within the space of two inches he creates graceful, well detailed images which seem to have a life of their own. Though his creations lack that fine detail of Tang Suguo's sculpture, they are still quite attractive. While Lin works, his brother–in–law may offer you tea and sing the praises of this young artist. The work of his hands can be seen around the room, including elegant court ladies who dangle flowing scarves with languid grace next to bold generals who raise their arms in a dramatic stance. After he completes his figures, Lin skewers them on bamboo sticks to dry. The final step is to mount the pieces on a black wooden base and cover them with glass lids, which may be somewhat roughly cut. His miniatures range in price from as little as 1 *yuan* up to 50 *yuan* for an elaborate dough landscape set within a half walnut shell. You may also find this young man's work for sale at the Beijing Hotel craft counter, but at somewhat higher prices.

If you visit Tang Suguo, you should try to visit Lin Chunxin as well, because this contrast provides an interesting insight into the differing approaches of a folk artist and fine artist working in the same medium. You can find Lin Chunxin in Beijing's Chongwen district at 45 Dongdan Santiao Street. Although he does not have a telephone, the sculptor will be happy to welcome visitors.

4. Rongbaozhai ★ ★
(Studio of Glorious Treasures)
19 W. Liulichang Street
Telephone: 330097 and 333352

荣宝斋
琉璃厂西宁19号

Manager: Cai Jinpeng

Hours: 9–6

Accepts traveler's checks and major credit cards

Has English–speaking staff

Recommended Crafts

- watercolor wood–block prints of camels or yaks by Wu Zuoren; graceful, fleet horses by Xu Beihong; delightfully eccentric renditions of Beijing opera figures by Guan Liang; and anything by Qi Baishi (10–50 *yuan*)
- stones for use as seals, of which those with uniquely patterned red or black veins are especially beautiful; look for those with charming carvings of lions, dragons or auspicious spirits on the top of the stone (5–50 *yuan*)
- small wood–block print albums with charming scenes of landscapes or languid beauties
- ceramic implements for the artist's desk, such as small notched brush rests, brush jars, paper weights for horizontal scrolls, or water dishes; these are often of blue–and–white underglazed decoration or pale green celadon (2–80 *yuan*)

Although the staff no longer greets customers with low bows and cups of steaming tea, Rongbaozhai remains a haven for artists and art–lovers who come from all over China and the world to search through the store's unique collection of art supplies and implements. As you look over handmade papers of sandalwood tree bark, rice straw, or silkworm cocoons you may be joined on one side by a famous painter searching for a special wolf and badger–hair brush and on the other side by a collector looking at brocade samples with which to mount a painting in the traditional hanging–scroll style. In another part of the store are sold an extraordinary collection of reproductions of paintings by most of China's greatest artists, including Qi Baishi, Xu Beihong, Li Kuchan, Li Keran and Wu Zuoren.

For over 200 years Rongbaozhai has been selling art supplies and watercolor wood–block prints to a faithful clientele. After recent renovations, the store reopened in late 1985 and is now once again thronged with amateur and professional Chinese artists, foreign collectors and tourists. Here it is possible not only to buy all the paraphernalia for producing a traditional landscape painting and have the piece bordered with brocade and mounted as a scroll, but also to order a seal carved with your name in Chinese for a finishing imprint on the painting.

The achievements of Chinese painting are intimately connected with the materials used in its composition. The fluid, suggestive landscapes with skeletal mountains against a graduated wash of sea require a firm but elastic brush which sweeps freely across fine, absorbent paper. Over the centuries Chinese painters have developed special brushes, paper, ink, and pigments which lend themselves best to the artist's bold imagination. Today Rongbaozhai carries almost every type of painting utensil and specializes in the "four treasures" of the artist's studio: brush, paper, ink stick, and inkstone.

Browsing artists here compare the textures of different pieces of absorbent *xuan* paper, which is still handmade in Anhui Province by a process which requires nearly 300 steps. The most popular brushes are those of wolf, badger, goat, rabbit, weasel, squirrel, or deer hair, depending on the style of stroke required in the work. The best ink continues to be made by burning tung oil or pine wood, adding glue and aromatics, and kneading the material before allowing it to dry slowly. The resultant dried cakes are ground at the time of use in a special indented stone carved of several varieties of smooth, fine grained rock. It is not unusual to see a Japanese or Hong Kong visitor paying several thousand *yuan* for a superior inkstone made of dense, fine grained mountainous rock from Guangdong Province. As you stand in this store full of knowledgeable and demanding Chinese testing the feel of brushes and the texture of papers, you will be struck by the realization that the long traditions of Chinese painting continue to be very much alive today.

Another specialty of Rongbaozhai is their water color wood–block prints. Monochrome wood–block prints were first produced in China in the 9th century and multicolor reproductions at the end of the 17th century. Today the wood–block printing workshop at Rongbaozhai represents a level of skill which raises the technique of printing to an art form. There are three steps in the printing process, known in Chinese as *mu–ban shui–yin.*

The first step is to trace the patterns of the original painting, giving meticulous attention to each detail of brushwork. In general, one block is reserved for each color, but a large area of color must sometimes be divided into several blocks. Those who do the tracing must themselves be master artists versant in the characteristic techniques and style of brushwork of the artist whose work they are reproducing. The second step is to paste the tracing on the block in reverse as a model and carve out the piece. The carver must study the original painting and then translate its every nuance with the blade of his knife. The most desirable types of wood for this work are hardwoods with a tight, fine grain, such as tu li (a wild, non fruit–bearing pear wood) or yellow poplar. The largest block is two feet wide. The third step is to print the block. A master copier selects the exact shade of wash required, brushes color on the block and then gently applies paper. The finishing touch is to mount the reproduction on heavier paper with wheat paste and border it with strips of silk brocade. Each of these stages can be seen in the workshops in the back of the store, were visitors are welcome. After witnessing this demanding process, one finds it easy to see why the identification of such reproductions as copies, rather than originals, sometimes confounds even experts.

5. National Art Gallery Shops ★ ★
Chaoyangmen Street at Wangfujing Street
Telephone: 441615

中国美术馆外宾服务部
王府井大丁

Manager: Liao Kaiming

Hours: 8:30–4, closed Monday

Accepts traveler's checks and major credit cards

No English–speaking staff

Recommended Crafts

(Because the merchandise varies, only a general recommendation can be made here.)
- any sculptures by "Clayman Zhang"
- folk art such as papercuts, painted clay toys and figurines, colorful prints of door gods, and peasant paintings
- distinctive crafts and reproductions such as Tang multicolor glazed ceramics, early bronzes, and Dunhuang clay sculptures
- innovative, one–of–a–kind works by younger artists

Housed in an attractive modern building with a roof of decorative yellow–glazed tile, the National Art Gallery displays art by young and old Chinese artists. The gallery has no permanent collection but mounts changing exhibitions, often including shows of foreign art. Even if you are not particularly interested in Chinese paintings, you may find a visit to the gallery's sales areas to be quite rewarding. And on a hot summer day it is nice to be able to relax for a moment outside in the quiet bamboo grove.

The National Art Gallery shops display a careful selection of unusual crafts and folk art, some of which are not available anywhere else in China. The manager and his staff choose pieces from all over China with a fine eye for quality and uniqueness. And the objects are not necessarily expensive. Furthermore, it is also possible to arrange commissions by painters, craftsmen, and sculptors whose works are on exhibit in the gallery. If you see something there that you like very much, you should inquire further in the shops.

There are two shops here, one located up the stairs at the entrance and then to the left on the main floor. The other is on the lower, street level inside the courtyard to the right as you face the building. Unlike larger stores, the merchandise here varies greatly from month to month. But you can always be sure to find unusual, well made art objects at reasonable prices. In addition to a large selection of paintings and prints, the shops have some interesting antique reproductions. On a recent visit we saw Tang multicolored glazed horses (30–90 *yuan*) from Luoyang, where the finest reproductions of this type are said to be made. A fine bronze reproduction of the famous Gansu horse, captured with hooves raised in mid–flight, was also available (500 *yuan*), along with red glazed Jun ware ceramic vases and small animals from Henan Province (around 70 *yuan*). We also saw brightly painted clay sculptures of fierce Buddhist guardian deities in the style of those of the Dunhuang caves (100 *yuan*), which we had not seen anywhere else.

If you like folk art, you may be able to find some unique pieces at the gallery shops. Traditional–style, ten–inch painted clay figures by the famous Tianjin folk artist known as "Clayman Zhang" can be found here for 30 *yuan*. Clay folk toys and colorful, wood–block print door gods from Beijing were also seen on a recent visit. A very fine set of Wuxi painted clay folk toys was only three *yuan* for a set of the three auspicious gods of prosperity, official position, and longevity (*fu lu shou*).

You may fall in love with the vigorous and colorful gouaches by peasant painters in Shanghai's Jinshan County and Shaanxi Province, which have been popular items here. Or you may choose papercuts in distinctive styles from various regions of China: sharp and vigorous designs with bold outlines from Shanxi, Shaanxi, and Shandong provinces in the north and delicate, intricately cut examples from the South. Foshan, near Guangzhou, produces exquisite, large, latticework–style papercuts of landscape scenes or floral patterns with hand painted detail.

The shops are willing to take a risk and stock innovative, experimental pieces by young artists just graduated from institutions such as the Central Academy of Fine Arts and the Central Academy of Arts and Crafts. This is somewhat unusual in China, where art selections are made more often by bureaucrats than by trained artists. If for no other reason than this, the gallery shops are worth a visit. You may, for example, be able to find unique new types of ceramics created by artists experimenting with glaze techniques, or you may find the work of a young artist yet to become famous.

Do not be misled by the initial impression of these shops. Although they are connected with an institution often visited by tourist groups, their merchandise is not the run–of–the–mill souvenir type, but is composed of fine quality art objects, often one–of–a–kind, which have been selected from the works of some of the best artists and craft workers in China. Also feel free to ask to see other examples in a particular style if you don't see exactly what you are looking for. Because the display area is somewhat limited, not everything can be shown at once, and the friendly staff is usually happy to bring out additional pieces from the back room.

6. Beijing Huaxia Arts and Crafts Shop ★ ★
(also called "Arts and Crafts Shop of Beijing Trust
Trade Company")
249 South Dongsi Road
(Moved to this location from 12 Chongwenmennei Street in late
1985; original site is being renovated and should re–open at the
end of 1987)
Telephone: 551529

华夏工艺品商店
东四南大于249 号

Hours: 8 a.m. to 10 p.m. daily

Manager: Chen Wenguang
Antiques expert: Ma Dianchen

Accepts traveler's checks and major credit cards

No English–speaking staff

Recommended Crafts

- old Japanese and European clocks
- old Yixing teapots (80–90 *yuan*)
- Cizhou ceramic pillows and figurines (60 *yuan* and up)
- embroidered opera costumes, such as a handsome yellow three–dragon robe worn for an imperial role (400–600 *yuan*)
- late Qing Dynasty embroidered vests and robes (60 *yuan* and up)
- old embroidered hats (5–20 *yuan*) and colorful multi–panel skirts
- glazed ceramic roof tiles with guardian figures

To veteran foreign residents and knowledgeable diplomatic staff in Beijing, a stop at Huaxia is one of life's pleasant pastimes. One old hand believes that this is the best shop in China and regrets that it is no longer a well kept "diplomatic secret." Over the years Huaxia, or the "theater shop" as it is commonly known by foreign residents, has served Beijing's foreign community. In this shop one catches a feeling of the Beijing of the 1920's and 30's. Here one can find not only antique Chinese furniture, carpets, porcelain and opera costumes, but antique European and Japanese clocks and watches, and other Western curios as well, an assortment which makes the shop unique.

Huaxia is one of a number of "commission" or second–hand stores that sell everything from spare parts, used cameras, television sets and radios to antique ceramics. The patient buyer willing to sort through a great deal of used miscellanea and modern bric–a–brac may eventually be rewarded by finding something quite extraordinary.

Beijing has had a long tradition of such second–hand shops and stalls. The Liulichang area was especially known for its vendors selling all manner of old books and paintings, antique ceramics and jade along with spurious modern imitations. Because some of the vendors in the past resorted to forceful methods of persuasion, these spots came to be known as "tiger shops." Today the visitor to Huaxia will be met with a friendlier reception by a staff who can arrange for purchases to be shipped overseas. But there is still an air of time standing still here, a feeling which finds expression in the huge collection of elaborate old European and Japanese clocks of all shapes and sizes, mute testament to the long passed fads and styles of fashionable Chinese and foreigners in a bygone Beijing.

This is one of the few places in China where you can buy old glazed roof tiles decorated with distinctive guardian figures, a beautiful architectural feature of Beijing's important old buildings such as the Forbidden City and Summer Palace. These charming figures of dragon, phoenix, lion, and celestial horse were arranged to deflect evil spirits from the vulnerable corners of a building; the higher the rank of the building's occupants, the more numerous were the figures. Exquisite silver and gold ornaments decorated with blue–green kingfisher feathers can be found here, as well as restored furniture, old wooden chests, and old carpets, a favorite of diplomatic representatives for decorating their quarters.

Handsome modern opera costumes are also available, such as a colorful three–dragon robe for 600 *yuan*. Or you can sort through the wide variety of late Qing textile pieces and gowns, including silk embroidered collars, panels, hats and robes. You may see several types of symbols on these embroidery pieces. One type uses a rebus or homophone which conveys a double meaning. A red bat, for example (*hong fu in Chinese*) is identified with "abundant good fortune" (also pronounced *hong fu*), while a deer (*lu*) represents the hope of attaining official position (*lu*). Round coins with square holes in the center symbolize the hope of future wealth, and peonies the hope of achieving wealth and high rank. Because the Chinese character for "seed" also means "sons," the many seeded pomegranate represents the wish for many sons to carry on the family name.

Some of these textiles have patterns decorated with the highly valued forbidden stitch, also known as the "Peking knot," which was made of a tiny ring formed by looping a thread around the needle before taking a stitch. It is said that the stitch was so intricate it was eventually banned because it caused blindness in the embroiderers. Textile pieces executed in this stitch became much sought after, and by the turn of this century such textiles were often cut up and sewn into separate panels. If you are lucky you may happen upon such a piece.

Ceramics, too, are a specialty of Huaxia. Look for fine old unglazed brown, or "purple sand," clay tea pots from the city of Yixing. These are decorated with an understated elegance of jointed bamboo stems, flowering plum boughs, gourds, or fruit, and have the wonderful patina of age and use that even exceptional modern pieces lack. Another distinctive type of ceramic you may find is the robust folk stoneware of Cizhou decorated with black or brown freestyle patterns of flowers, babies, animals or fish on a white or tan ground. Old ceramic pillows with chubby baby boys holding lotuses symbolize a wish for the birth of a succession of sons to carry on the family name, while fish represent abundance. Although these wares are not as well known as some of the other ceramic families, Cizhou folk stonewares have a vigor and charming directness which make them especially appealing to people today.

Note: A branch of Huaxia at 293 Wangfujing (telephone: 551819) sells contemporary crafts, clothing, table cloths, and a lesser selection of the pieces mentioned above. Business hours are 9:00 a.m. to 9:30 p.m.

7. Rosefinch Palace of Arts ★ ★

51 Xizhimennei Avenue at Xinjiekou Street
Telephone: 664583

朱雀艺术宫
西直门内大于51号
（ 新于口）

Manager: Zhou Guojin

Hours: 9–6 daily

Accepts traveler's checks but no credit cards

No English–speaking staff

Recommended Crafts

- beautifully embroidered Miao squares (10–15 *yuan*) and costume pieces (35 *yuan* and up)
- brightly painted clay toys (1–5 *yuan*)
- finely embroidered tiger pillows (10–15 *yuan*)

Rosefinch Palace of Arts is a unique store dedicated to promoting all types of folk art from all over China. The visitor here will be charmed by a colorful amalgam of embroidered animal pillows, clay toys, batik clothing, dough figures, and a hundred other kinds of folk art. The store was founded in October of 1985 by 50 graduates of the 1952 class of the Central College of Fine Arts. These people, many of whom are now famous figures in the Chinese art world, felt that not enough attention was being paid to the country's folk art and minority crafts. The store they founded is one of the very few in China which specialize in folk art.

You will find it a pleasure to shop here with the assistance of an extremely enthusiastic and knowledgeable staff who can give you background information about how the crafts are made and the people who make them. Prices are quite reasonable and many of the pieces are underpriced. Some of the things to look for are colorful, appliquéd vests for children, papercuts, finely embroidered pillows in the shape of tigers, batiks of all sorts, dough figures, and embroidered Miao squares and clothing pieces.

Recommended Stores ★

1. Beijing Opera Costume Factory Retail Shop ★
130 Qianmen Street
Telephone: 753269 (factory); 752853 (retail shop)

戏剧服装厂门市部
前门大于130 号

Factory Director: Wang Jie

Hours: 9–6 daily

Accepts only cash

No English–speaking staff

Recommended Crafts

- cloth practice slippers (3–5 *yuan*)
- stage props such as swords or daggers (15–25 *yuan*)
- embroidered, imperial–style robes (100 *yuan* and up)

This is the shop where the famous Chinese performers of Beijing opera go for all their costumes and stage props. The factory has been clothing opera stars since the 1940's. Today there are 500 workers who will embroider colorful costumes for any role, providing everything from headdresses to cloth shoes and all props. The historical costumes for period dramas on Chinese television also come from this shop, where master costume maker, Mr. Shao, has been working for 47 years and learned the craft from his father. Look for inexpensive cloth practice shoes or stage props such as swords and small daggers, as well as the bright, intricately embroidered imperial dragon robes. The shop will also make costumes to order and repair old costumes.

2. Jingdezhen Art Porcelain Service Company ★
149 Qianmen Street
Telephone: 332613 and 334452

景德镇艺术瓷器服务部
前门大于149号

Manager: Guo Hongji

Hours: 9–6 daily

Accepts traveler's checks but not credit cards

No English–speaking staff

Recommended Crafts

- "eggshell" porcelain bowls (200–800 *yuan*)
- set of blue–and–white underglazed ceramic pieces for the artist's desk (95 *yuan*)

The kilns of Jingdezhen, China's porcelain capital, produced the exquisite wares which graced the courts of Chinese emperors, Arabian princes and European kings for over a thousand years. In 1369 the first Ming emperor set aside the kilns in Jingdezhen solely for imperial use. From that time on almost all the porcelain for the Ming and Qing courts was supplied by these imperial kilns. The city soon eclipsed all the other ceramic centers in China, and in the early years of trade with Europe almost all export porcelain came from this small city as well. Today the Jingdezhen kilns continue to produce fine porcelains, and this shop is their biggest direct distributor in Beijing. Here you can get a complete 54–piece dinner service for 48 *yuan* or exquisitely fine walled "eggshell" porcelain bowls for 200–800 *yuan*. The selection is vast and the prices are quite good. Look for a beautiful set of blue–and–white under-glazed ceramic pieces for an artist's desk, containing brush or pencil jar, paper weight, and water dish (95 *yuan*). If you are looking for Jingdezhen porcelain, this is the place to go for a large selection, high quality, and reasonable prices.

3. Beijing Arts and Crafts Service Department ★
200 Wangfujing Street
Telephone: 557579

工艺美术服务部
王府井大于200 号

Manager: Chen Feng

Hours: 8:30 a.m. – 10 p.m. daily

Accepts traveler's checks and all major credit cards; there is also a counter to exchange money on the third floor, which is open only to foreigners

Has English–speaking staff

Recommended Crafts

- Weifang wood–block print kites (15–30 *yuan*)
- leather shadow figures (10–15 *yuan*)
- blue and white qipao (20 *yuan*)

Located on busy Wangfujing street, this store is always crowded with Chinese and foreigners visiting the capital. On the first two floors are a broad variety of crafts, art supplies, clothing, and toys. The foreign visitor will get some feeling for Chinese tastes and lifestyle by shopping here. On a recent visit, for example, I found young Chinese were crowded around a second floor counter selling the gold jewelry which has become a new craze in China.

Look for colorful Weifang wood–block print kites, small cloth and clay toys, painted leather shadow figures of Chinese opera characters, and robust stoneware teapots and cooking jars. A blue and white stencil print *qipao*, or traditional Manchu dress with side slits and assymetrical neck closing, was another attractive item sold here.

4. Brocade Box Factory Shop ★

Qianmen, 40 Langfang Toutiao Lane
Telephone: 331508 (workshop); 330613 (sales department)

锦盒厂门市部
前门外廊房头条40号

Manager: Hua Shulin

Hours: 8–5 daily

Accepts traveler's checks and major credit cards

No English–speaking staff

Recommended Crafts

- jewelry cases (20 *yuan*)
- curved boxes with handles (8 *yuan*)
- boxes to hold tea sets or art supplies

Located off a narrow, bustling street in the Dashanlan shopping area, the "Box Shop," as it is known, is a specialized store for collectors or others needing fine brocade boxes. For over a hundred years craftsmen in this neighborhood have been making brocade boxes with traditional bone pick and cloth closings. This shop has been in existence for over 50 years and is the only store of its kind in Beijing. While the clientele of earlier years included emperors, today's customers are mostly Chinese out–of–towners visiting Beijing. Do not be deterred by the small display area. When you go upstairs to the workshops you will find boxes lying everywhere, crammed into every corner. Virtually any size or shape of box can be gotten here, and if the staff does not have it, they will make it to order. One of their recent creations was an extraordinary three–foot box in the shape of the Empress Dowager's marble boat at the Summer Palace.

Prices are excellent, the shop is geared to producing in quantity, and the staff will also arrange for shipment abroad. Look for jewelry cases with small drawers or boxes made to contain tea sets or art supplies such as chops, inksticks or inkstones. Some of the small, curved brocade boxes with handles might make nice evening bags, too. The store has a few traditional–style dolls dressed in silk costumes and crowned with elaborate headdresses. And you can always buy that marble boat.

5. Xidan Chopstick Store ★
160 N. Xidan Street
Telephone: 662729

西单筷子商店
西单北大于160 号

Deputy Manager: Guan Zhiqiang

Hours: 8:30 a.m. – 7:30 p.m. daily

Accepts cash only

No English–speaking staff

Recommended Crafts

- pair of silver chopsticks (60 *yuan*)
- lacquer chopsticks (10 *yuan*)
- carved canes

The Xidan Chopstick Store is the only store in Beijing specializing in chopsticks from all over China. Because of the nature of the merchandise, few foreign visitors come here to shop. It is fascinating to watch the store's customers, many of whom are Chinese newlyweds just setting up housekeeping, trying out different pairs of chopsticks in order to find the perfect look and feel.

Prices are quite good here, ranging from as little as 1 *yuan* for a dozen simple bamboo chopsticks to 60 *yuan* for a pair of silver or ivory chopsticks. The range is enormous, including painted, carved, and lacquered chopsticks of bamboo and several kinds of wood, as well as chopsticks of silver, ivory, and a jade–like local green stone. Also look for carved canes and fragrant sandalwood fans from Suzhou, which are available in the summer for 20 *yuan*.

Occasionally Western newspapers report that the Chinese have given up using chopsticks in favor of Western utensils. One trip to this store will lay that myth to rest.

6. Artistic Red Lantern Factory Shop ★
Chongwen District, 348 East Zhushikou Street
(The factory is located at 328 East Zhushikou Street.)
Telephone: 751337 (shop); 752062 (office)

美术红灯厂门市部
崇文区珠市口东大于348 号

Hours: 8–5:30, closed Thursday

Accepts traveler's checks and major credit cards

No English–speaking staff

Recommended Crafts

- painted silk lanterns with black frames: medium (30 *yuan*) and large (70 *yuan*)
- red silk lanterns (20–30 *yuan*)

The Artistic Red Lantern Factory, located in what was once Beijing's pearl market district, is a testament to the enduring Chinese love for lanterns. In earlier years lanterns were the chief attraction of the New Year holiday which came at the middle of the first lunar month. During this holiday, known as the Lantern Festival, brightly colored lanterns of all shapes and sizes were alight in almost every home. Kindling the lanterns was thought to bring light and heat back to the world at the end of the long winter.

Imperial mansions and noble households were lit by costly and elaborate "palace lanterns" fashioned of silk or glass panels over frames of mahogany, boxwood, or sandalwood. Peasant families created less costly but equally colorful versions from panels of oiled paper, silk, or sheepskin fastened to bases of wood, bamboo, wire or rice stalks. Paintings, embroidery, or papercuts were added to the outside of these lanterns for a bold, festive touch. Wandering strollers carried lovely lanterns with tassels, pearl ornaments, bright feathers, or jade pendants which tinkled with each movement. There were also moving lanterns such as the famous "galloping horse lanterns" (*zou–ma deng*) which revolved with the heat of a candle placed inside.

Today the Red Lantern Factory, which also has a retail branch on Liulichang Street, still sells "palace lanterns" of silk and glass to local embassies, as well as to hotels and restaurants all over China and abroad. The factory will make lanterns to order, and it is likely that many of the lanterns you have seen in Chinese restaurants across the United States originated in this factory. There is an extensive selection here and prices are very reasonable. Look for hand painted lanterns on white silk with black wooden frames and red hanging tassels. The store also has elegant, round, red silk lanterns. You may be able to visit the workshops by special arrangement.

7. Donghuamen Furniture Shop ★
38 S. Dongsi Street
Telephone: 552693

东华门家具修理店
东四南大于38号

Manager: Jia Wencai

Hours: 9:30–6 daily

Accepts traveler's checks but no credit cards

No English–speaking staff

Recommended Crafts

- carved red lacquer chests (250 *yuan*)
- reproductions of small antique chests (120 *yuan*)

Over the centuries Chinese furniture has been sought after for its high level of workmanship and aesthetics. The finest furniture was made of a number of varieties of dark, close–grained woods imported from India, the Philippines and Southeast Asia. Over 30 types of rosewood alone were used to craft screens, chairs, tables, chests, and cabinets. Mahogany and gingko have also been used, while camphor wood, with its insect–repelling fragrance, was desirable for storage chests. Most highly regarded are the "Ming–style" objects, masterpieces of under-stated elegance translated into fluid, imaginative shapes. There is a timeless beauty to these chairs, tables, and chests which avoid the intrusive ornamentation marring later pieces.

Today the knowledgeable traveler can still find some of these elegant old pieces as well as faithful modern reproductions in several Beijing shops, one of which is the Dongsi Furniture Shop. This shop specializes in old, restored furniture and traditional chests. Its new pieces are made nearby at the Zhangshi Furniture Factory. On a recent visit we found antique black–lacquer tables inlaid with mother–of–pearl (500 *yuan*), and carved red lacquer chests. Also popular are the store's old camphor wood "three–width" chests which are extra wide and have three storage sections (300–800 *yuan*). Look for plain, classical chests with semicircular brass hinges, as well as reproductions of small antique chests.

It is a sad fact that young Chinese couples today look for more ostentatious, Western–influenced styles in furniture. There is, in fact, a phrase, "48–legs," which describes the recent craze of soon to be married brides for acquiring as many pieces of furniture as possible, including a sofa, table, desk, bookcase, and chairs—totalling 48 legs between them. The number of required legs has continued to grow with economic prosperity, and young people seem increasingly to want only Western–style designs. If you go to the back room of the Donghuamen, you will find it full of not very tasteful modern–looking wall units and suites of furniture surrounded by admiring young couples and newlyweds. We can only hope that the classical styles will not be entirely forgotten in the eager rush for new things.

8. Beixinqiao ★

30 N. Dongsi Street
Telephone: 445191

北新桥信托商店
东四北大亍30号

Manager: Yang Baozhen

Hours: 8–7 daily

Accepts cash only

No English–speaking staff

Recommended Crafts

• pair of antique hardwood chairs (360 *yuan*)

Beixinqiao is an interesting old second–hand shop which specializes in antique and restored old chairs and chests. There is always a lot of activity here, with people bringing in used furniture for resale or restoration. In some corners the chairs are piled to the ceiling. If you did not find what you wanted at Donghuamen, you might be luckier here.

On a recent visit we found a pair of fine, restored, antique hardwood chairs.

9. Palace Museum Souvenir Shop ★
Located just inside the rear entrance to the Forbidden City at the Gate of Divine Military Prowess (Shenwumen)
Telephone: 555031 ext. 545

故宫博物院外宾服务部
故宫博物院后部，神武门内

Manager: Wang Yushu

Hours: 8–4:30 daily

Accepts cash only; money can be exchanged there

Store is open to foreigners only

Has English–speaking staff

Recommended Crafts

- celadon bowls (8 *yuan*)
- reproductions of Cizhou ceramics
- small books of rubbings (5–12 *yuan*)

For the lover of Chinese art, the 500 year–old Forbidden City must certainly be the first stop on any Beijing itinerary. Once the home of China's emperors and families, the palace is now a public museum—the Palace Museum. This magnificent, walled city was designed to represent the universe in microcosm, with the emperor unmoving at its heart like the polestar at the center of the heavens. Today the 9,000 rooms house a vast collection of treasures from many periods of Chinese history, and each room seems more impressive than the next. Paintings, ceramics, bronzes, stone sculptures—all are here to marvel at.

At the rear of the Forbidden City, in one of the imperial resting pavilions, is the Palace Museum Souvenir Shop. The shop specializes in fine quality reproductions of paintings and crafts found in the Forbidden City, most of which are made in workshops on the palace grounds. Although the number of objects available at any time is rather limited, you may be able to find some unusual items. On past trips we have seen beautiful celadon bowls incised with floral or dragon designs for only 8 yuan, reproductions of robust brown and cream Cizhou ceramics as well as elegant Yixing teapots. Small books of rubbings make lovely, inexpensive gifts.

10. Marco Polo Carpet Shop ★

Agricultural Exhibition Hall
North Donghuan Road, Eastern Suburbs
Telephone: 582331, ext. 259

懋隆地毯商店
全国农业展览馆
东郊东环北路

Manager: Wang Baoping

Hours: 9–11:30 a.m. and 1:30–5 p.m. daily

Accepts traveler's checks and all major credit cards

Has English–speaking staff

Recommended Crafts

- sculpted Beijing carpets (12'x 15' for 2,400 *yuan*)
- old Xinjiang and Mongolian carpets
- silk carpets from Sichuan

If you want to leave China with a spectacular carpet, then the Marco Polo Carpet Shop is the place to come. For years Chinese carpets have been prized for their muted colors and restrained elegance. Fragments of woolen carpets buried in the desert sands of western China for 1,800 years have recently been unearthed in astonishingly good condition. Beijing craftsmen today continue to make lustrous, deep pile carpets knotted by hand.

The Marco Polo carpet shop carries an impressive variety of rugs from Beijing as well as most of the other important rug centers in China—Mongolia, Xinjiang, and Chengdu. (No rugs from Tianjin were available on a recent visit, however.) Materials include silk, camel hair, wool, and even human hair. The weaving process is lengthy and demanding. The craft workers begin by knotting woolen yarns onto strong, cotton warp threads. Thread by thread, row by row, the workers loop, knot and cut the woolen yarn. After the body of the carpet is complete, the pile is sculpted with embossed designs. Then it is washed in chemical baths to mute the colors and create a soft, lustrous surface.

Among the attractions at the Marco Polo Shop are its huge floor space, clear displays and knowledgeable, English–speaking staff, who are happy to arrange for shipments abroad. A 12' by 15' carpet costs about 200 *yuan* to ship to the United States, for example, excluding insurance fees. The manager told us he estimated that carpets purchased here average about one–third what they would cost in the US. We recently saw beautiful sculpted 12' by 15' Beijing carpets in muted pastel tones for 2,400 *yuan*, as well as old Xinjiang and Mongolian carpets.

When making your final selection, you should remember that the best Chinese carpets have a 5/8" pile. Beijing rugs are somewhat softer and less durable than those produced in Tianjin, and so the latter are usually more expensive. If you are planning to buy an antique carpet, you should ask the store manager to verify on the sales receipt that the rug is an "antique, over 100 years old." This will clarify the term "antique" and should qualify you to bring the carpet through US customs duty free.

11. Chinese Arts and Crafts Trade Fair ★
Beijing Exhibition Center
135 Xiwai Street, 2 East Pavilion
Telephone: 890541 ext. 462 and 463

中国工艺美术品展销会
北京展览馆东二馆
西外大于135 号

Manager: Zhang Ximin

Hours: 9–5 daily

Accepts traveler's checks and all major credit cards

Has English–speaking staff

Recommended Crafts

- celadon vases (60–120 *yuan*)
- Fuzhou bodiless lacquer vases (300 *yuan*)
- Weifang kites (20 *yuan*)

• clay toys (2 *yuan*)

In the words of its manager, the Chinese Arts and Crafts Trade Fair displays the best arts and crafts to be found throughout China, from inexpensive folk toys to $25,000 ivory sculptures. The large, attractive floor area contains clear displays and a huge variety of items, including gemstone carvings, contemporary museum–quality crafts, and fine reproductions. One of the nice things about this shop is that its ceramic wares are grouped according to the kiln system or region of production, which makes a valuable introduction to the sometimes confusing array of Chinese ceramics. You may choose pale–green incised celadon vases for 60–120 *yuan* or pay 22,000 *yuan* for a creamy white award–winning *blanc–de–Chine* statue of the Buddhist goddess Guanyin, made in the old porcelain center of Dehua in Fujian Province.

You can also find feather–light bodiless lacquer vases from Fuzhou (300 *yuan*) and framed double–sided embroideries from Suzhou (400–3,000 *yuan*), some of which are made with a different animal on each side. For 55,000 *yuan* you can take home a huge, elaborate Guangdong ivory carving which incorporates 41 concentrically carved spheres. If, on the other hand, you are looking for a more modest purchase, the shop carries small, local clay figures for 2 *yuan*, colorful kites from Weifang in Shangdong Province (20 *yuan*) and shadow figures from Shaanxi Province (9–22 *yuan*).

For the traveler with very limited time in China who wants to get a taste of the diversity of contemporary Chinese crafts and folk arts, the Arts and Crafts Trade Fair is well worth a stop.

12. Yuanlong Embroidery Silk Store ★
55 Tiantan Road, Second floor
Telephone: 754059

元隆顾绣绸缎商行
天坛路55号2 楼

Manager: Wang Fengmin

Hours: 9–7:30 daily

Accepts traveler's checks and major credit cards

Has English–speaking staff

Recommended Crafts

- raw silk (5 *yuan*/meter)
- brocade jackets (70 *yuan*)
- down–filled silk quilts (200 *yuan*)

One ounce of silk worm eggs produces 30,000 worms, which consume a ton of mulberry leaves to create twelve pounds of raw silk. China had already begun to export her silks to the Middle East 2,500 years ago, across the caravan trails which in later years were to become known as the Silk Road. The route stretched from the old capitol of Changan (present–day Xian) for 7,000 kilometers to Syria on the Mediterranean. The trip was immensely dangerous. Travelers had to cross treacherous mountain passes and desert wastes through territories of hostile nomadic tribes. The caravans could manage the trip only with the aid of Bactrian camels, which could smell water in the sand and were reputed to give warning of coming sandstorms. In the best of times the trip took ten months to a year. Today it is not so difficult to acquire China's prized fabrics, and the visitor to Beijing can spend many pleasant hours looking through a tremendous selection of every kind of silk at the Yuanlong Embroidery Silk Store.

The Yuanlong Silk shop was established 100 years ago expressly to provide fine silks to Beijing's foreign community. It used to be located on Zhushikou Street, which was known to foreign residents as Embroidery Street, but is now located in bright, new quarters near the Temple of Heaven. The store's fabrics come from the best embroidery and silk–producing regions of China, including Zhejiang, Jiangsu and Sichuan Provinces, Hangzhou, Suzhou, Nanjing, and Shanghai. You can find just about any kind of silk by the yard here, from nubby raw silks to damasks, satins, brocades, and exquisite gauzes woven with satin panels. Raw silk is an especially good buy, available in a rainbow of colors for as little as 5 *yuan* per meter, considerably below international prices. (It is advisable to check for shrinkage and dye fastness before you begin to work with the fabric, however.) Some finished silk garments are also available, such as pyjamas, shirts, and bright brocade jackets. Huge down–filled silk quilts are also very reasonable. The store has new and old embroideries and silk carpets from Sichuan Province. If you have time in Beijing, the store will make garments to order for you.

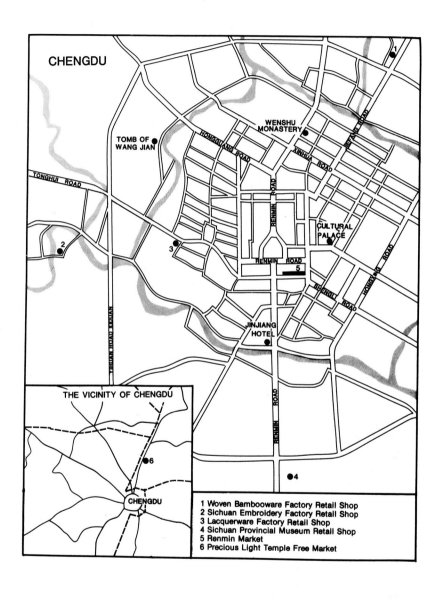

CHENGDU

TOMB OF
WANG JIAN

WENSHU
MONASTERY

HONGGUANG ROAD

XINHUA ROAD

TONGHUI ROAD

RENMIN ROAD

CULTURAL
PALACE

RENMIN ROAD

SHENGLI ROAD

DONGFENG ROAD

JINJIANG
HOTEL

SICHUAN ROAD

RENMIN ROAD

THE VICINITY OF CHENGDU

CHENGDU

1 Woven Bambooware Factory Retail Shop
2 Sichuan Embroidery Factory Retail Shop
3 Lacquerware Factory Retail Shop
4 Sichuan Provincial Museum Retail Shop
5 Renmin Market
6 Precious Light Temple Free Market

Chengdu

Chengdu, the capital of Sichuan Province, is located on a broad, fertile plain which is one of the most densely populated and agriculturally productive areas in China. It is surrounded by lush, green rice paddies and fields which turn into a sea of flowering, yellow rape plants in late spring. The Chengdu plain still receives water through a vast water conservancy project with a dam, drainage system, and irrigation canals first built in the 3rd century BC and reconstructed periodically in the years following.

Chengdu has a long history and was established as capital of the Kingdom of Shu during the Three Kingdoms Period (220–316). The city is well known for its lacquerware and silk brocade, both of which were already highly developed industries by the Han Dynasty. Because of its reputation for silk weaving, Chengdu was called the "City of Brocade." The city has preserved much of its traditional culture, from tea house performances by story tellers to local opera and puppet theater. The region is also well known for a variety of crafts. When he visited Chengdu in the 13th century, Marco Polo noted that the vendors set up their stalls near the bridges within the city. "All along the bridges on either side are rows of booths devoted to the practice of various forms of trade and craft. They are wooden structures, erected every morning and taken down at night." (Latham, p. 170.) Today as you walk along the narrow side streets of the city, you will see clusters of shops and free markets specializing in one kind of product, as was the custom in China for centuries. One street sells hardware, one has daily–use ceramics, one sells vegetables, and another displays all manner of baskets.

What to Look For

Visitors to Chengdu will find an array of fine crafts available in the city's stores, factory retail outlets, and free markets. Painted lacquerware is an ancient specialty of Chengdu, as are silk embroidery and brocade. Local artisans are skilled at weaving straw and bamboo into a variety of patterns for use in purses, mats, and baskets. Most distinctive are the porcelain tea sets and vases covered with fine threads of bamboo woven into exquisite patterns. Locally made silver and gold filigree jewelry is currently very popular with Chinese buyers, while foreign tourists seem to favor the minority folk jewelry available in local shops.

Tibetan swords, knives, saddles, bags, shoes, and clothing are all interesting crafts which can be found in Chengdu, reflecting the sizable Tibetan population of the province. Another distinctive facet of local art is the vivid scenes which decorate many Han Dynasty tomb tiles and bricks in the region. The designs were made by pressing wooden blocks into the moist clay before it was fired. Whether depicting hunters shooting ducks beside a stream teeming with fat fish, farmers reaping grain, or a bustling market scene, these pictures are unforgettable in their expressive simplicity and vigor. Rubbings made from these designs are popular craft items in Chengdu today.

Where to Look

The recommended craft stores and factory outlets described below are spread about in various parts of the city. In the busy downtown center at Yanshikou Street are the various shops of the Renmin (People's) Market. If you go west on Shengli Road you will come to the Lacquerware Factory, while the Sichuan Embroidery Factory is located farther west, near the Thatched Hut of Du Fu. The Sichuan Brocade Factory is also located near the Thatched Hut of Du Fu, at 5 East Caotang Road (Tel: 25667). Although the factory has only a small room for retail sales and a rather limited selection of brocades, some visitors may want to stop here for a look.

The Provincial Museum is south of the city heart on Renmin Road. Going northeast on Jiefang Road brings you to the Bamboo Articles Factory. The Baoguang Temple is 10 miles north of Chengdu in Xindu County. At night you may want to stroll along South Renmin Road near the Jinjiang Guest House, where vendors sell a variety of inexpensive paintings, daily–use items, clothing, and woven straw, rattan, and bamboo goods.

Recommended Stores ★

1. Woven Bambooware Factory Retail Shop ★
12 Jiefang Road, Section 1
Telephone: 32421

竹编工艺厂门市部
解放路一段12号

Head of Reception Department: Xiao Suhua

Hours: 8:30–6 daily

Accepts traveler's checks but no credit cards

Has English–speaking staff

Recommended Crafts

- objects of bamboo woven over porcelain, including small ginger jars and vases (8 *yuan*), wine sets, and tea sets (100 *yuan*)
- zippered purses of woven bamboo (8–9 *yuan*)

This factory is a good source for the finely woven bamboo vases and containers which are a specialty of Chengdu. The bamboo used is a special variety found in the Qionglai Mountains west of Chengdu, one of the native habitats of the rare Giant panda. Each length of bamboo is carefully split into fine threads which are colored and woven into decorative patterns for use as baskets, trays, purses, stacking boxes, and place mats.

Another distinctive craft you will find here is constructed of fine bamboo threads woven in intricate patterns over porcelain bodies. This combination of bamboo weaving with porcelain bases from the famous kilns of Jingdezhen has a 100–year history in Chengdu. You can find beautiful vases, ginger jars, teapots, tea cups, and wine sets made by this method. Some pieces look strikingly modern with their sparse use of color and intricate woven designs, while others call to mind the bold designs of American Indian pottery. Prices are quite reasonable, ranging from 0.50 *yuan* for a simple bamboo place mat, 1 *yuan* for a woven jewelry case, and 8 *yuan* for a small flower vase or ginger jar. You may find a complete tea set, including teapot, six cups and saucers, and serving tray for 100 *yuan*. Small woven purses of various sizes are available for 8 to 9 *yuan*.

2. **Sichuan Embroidery Factory Retail Shop** ★
   Located on the road running east of the Thatched Hut of Du Fu
   (Caotang Dong Lu)
   Telephone: 24383

蜀绣厂门市部
草堂东路

Hours: 8 a.m. – 10 p.m. daily

Accepts traveler's checks but no credit cards

Has English–speaking staff; translators not available for tour of factory

Recommended Crafts

- embroidered silk scarves (15–20 *yuan*)
- embroidered wall hanging with character for long life (50 *yuan*)
- single–sided embroidery of carp, flowers, women or landscapes (25–1,500 *yuan*)
- double–sided embroidery of pandas or flowers (450–10,000 *yuan*)

Shu or Sichuan embroidery is one of China's four famous styles of embroidery, distinguished by its realistic detail and its neat and tight stitches executed in luminous threads. Visitors will find it interesting to see the embroiderers at work making single–sided embroidery pictures of landscape scenes, flowers, elegant court ladies, or carp. Today the needleworkers have added double–sided techniques to their repertoire, producing works of giant pandas, monkeys, and cranes, although these pieces do not quite seem to equal those of Suzhou for exquisite detail. Presented in square or round frames of rosewood or mahogany, with intricate latticework stands, these double–sided pictures are charming nevertheless. The factory also produces some embroidered costumes for the local opera (85 *yuan* and up) and embroidered bed and table linens. After touring the factory, visitors may stop at the small exhibition hall which displays a variety of needlework products. Purchases can be made in an adjacent sales room attended by a friendly, eager, staff.

3. Lacquerware Factory Retail Shop ★
625 West Shengli Road
Telephone: 27681

漆器厂门市部
胜利西路625 号

Hours: 8–5 daily, (closed every afternoon from 12–1:30)

Accepts cash only

Has English–speaking staff

Recommended Crafts

- jewelry case (9 *yuan*)
- square tray (30 *yuan*)
- vases (60–169 *yuan*, depending on the size)
- candy tray in the shape of a flower, with eight inner compartments (100 *yuan*)

The creation of graceful vessels with painted designs on a lacquer surface was already a highly developed craft in China over 2,000 years ago. At that time the production of lacquerware was an important craft industry carefully controlled by the state, with Sichuan as its center. At two imperial workshops here ancient artisans fashioned costly trays, cups, and boxes painted with fluid motifs of dancing birds and upright dragons holding bows and arrows. The craft was highly specialized, and as many as eight craftsmen were needed to complete one piece. Separate workers fashioned the wooden base, processed the lacquer, applied the lacquer coatings, made the metal fittings, added the decoration, in-scribed the article, and completed the final polishing. One artisan was in charge of the overall work, and numerous officials oversaw the work-shops, adding their names to the list of contributing craftsmen inscribed on each ware. In 1971 several hundred such lacquer pieces were discovered in the tomb of a Han Dynasty noblewoman buried at Mawang-dui, near Changsha in Hunan Province.

Today visitors to the Chengdu Lacquerware Factory can see modern craftsmen making reproductions of these lovely vessels as well as modern designs. After viewing the workshops, visitors may choose from a variety of reasonably priced items at the factory retail shop. In addition to reproductions of bronze boxes and lacquer pieces excavated from ancient tombs, you can find distinctive stacking boxes, plates, and jewelry cases, many of which are decorated with inlaid gold and silver wire. Painted lacquer boxes and plates decorated with designs found on Han tomb bricks are another popular craft item here.

4. Sichuan Provincial Museum Retail Shop ★
279 South Renmin Road, Section Four
(Shop is located on the second floor)
Telephone: 25907, 22158

四川博物馆外宾服务部
人民南路四段279 号

Hours: 8:30–11:30 a.m. and 2–5 p.m. daily

Accepts cash only

Has English–speaking staff

Recommended Crafts

- unglazed Han tomb figures (60–80 *yuan*)
- glazed tea set (10 *yuan*)
- polychrome glazed Tang horses, made in Luoyang (10–80 *yuan*)
- rubbings of Han Dynasty tomb bricks and tiles with hunting or farming scenes (15–20 *yuan*)

The Sichuan Provincial Museum has an interesting collection of tomb figures, decorated bricks and tiles, and Buddhist statues which have been excavated in the province. The museum also has a small shop which sells reproductions of pieces in the museum collection. The majority of these items are ceramic reproductions and rubbings. The items available will vary greatly depending on the time of the visit. On a recent trip we found reproductions of Han Dynasty unglazed tomb figurines, glazed tea sets, and polychrome glazed Tang horses from Luoyang. A nice selection of rubbings made from Han tomb tiles and bricks was also available.

5. Free market at the Precious Light Temple (Baoguang Si) ★
Northern suburbs of Chengdu, in Xindu County

宝光寺自由市场
宝光寺成都市北郊新都县

Hours: variable, but generally open 8:30 a.m. to 10:30 p.m.; the temple is open from 8–6 daily

Accepts cash only

No English–speaking vendors

Recommended Crafts

- baskets, shoes, bags, mats, and covered containers made of woven straw, bamboo, and rattan (1–30 *yuan*)

If you visit the Baoguang Temple with its white jade Buddha, statues of Buddhist perfected beings, paintings, calligraphy, and musical instruments, you may find it interesting to stroll through the free market located just outside the entrance to the temple. Here local farmers come to sell their homemade crafts, including baskets, shoes, bags, mats, and covered containers made of woven straw, bamboo, and rattan. Prices are extremely reasonable and bargaining is expected.

6. Renmin Market ★
At Yanshikou Street in downtown Chengdu
Telephone: 43842 (central exchange)

人民市场
盐市口

Hours: 9 – 6

Accepts cash only

Has no English–speaking staff

Recommended Crafts

- colorful woven sashes worn by Tibetan women (13 *yuan*)
- saddle sets (500 *yuan*)
- sets of clothing worn by Tibetan men (80 *yuan*)

The small shops of the Renmin Market are a good source for minority costumes and crafts. Here you can find Tibetan women's sashes, saddle sets, hats, and decorative knives and swords. On a recent visit we also saw complete sets of clothing worn by Tibetan men.

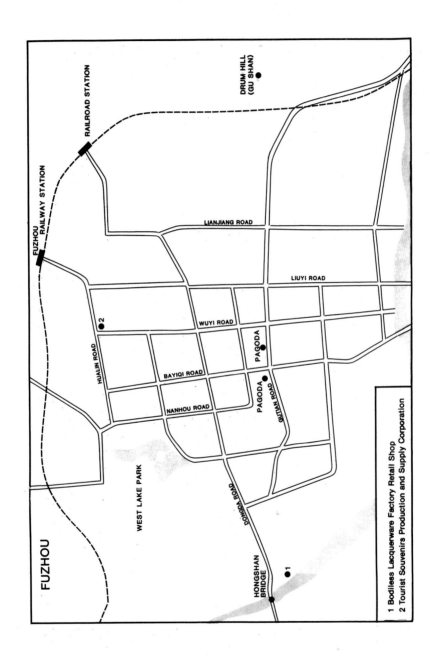

Fuzhou

Located along the curving coast of southeast China, Fujian Province faces the island of Taiwan across a narrow 100–mile strait. The province is largely mountainous, with five major ranges which run parallel to the coast from northeast to southwest. The Min and Jiulong Rivers, in the north and south respectively, cut through the ranges at a right angle, providing the major form of transport and communication. Junks and sampans still dot their waters, probably little changed in the 700 years since Marco Polo described them clustered in Fujian's southern ports. It was vessels such as these which carried China's prized silks, porcelain, and tea to Fujian's bustling eastern ports of Fuzhou (the present–day capital), Quanzhou, and Xiamen (Amoy). From there the luxury goods went all over the world to India, Africa, Persia and Arabia.

The Western rage for silk was matched only by its passion for porcelain, and it has been estimated that more than 60 million pieces were carried to the West by the year 1800. Europe's first shipment of tea arrived from China through Dutch ports in 1610. Some of the most precious varieties came from the Wuyi Mountains northwest of Fuzhou. The fragrant and mellow semi–fermented black tea was known in Europe as Bohea, after the name for these mountains in the local dialect. Today oolong varieties known as "Scarlet Robe" and "White Coxcomb" grow high on the mountain slopes in plots shielded from the harsh glare of the midday sun. The natives of Fujian consume these teas in tiny, thimble–sized cups; each mouthful is to be savored. The importance of the province in the history of the tea trade cannot be overrated, and many of the Western terms connected with this drink, from Bohea and pekoe to the word "tea" itself, derive from the local Fujian dialects.

Although the fertile southeastern corridor of the province historically provided an abundance of native produce, the difficult, mountainous terrain of the interior hindered transport to the poorer north and western regions of the province. Inland villages were self–contained and isolated, while the province as a whole had limited access to the rest of the country. The restricted travel and communication lead to the preservation of ancient forms of language, art, and social customs long after these were lost in other areas of China. Today the province presents fascinating material for studying the development of the Chinese language, traditional performing arts, such as opera and puppetry, and old forms of crafts and architecture.

The people of Fujian and Fuzhou are fiercely proud of their cultural heritage, rightfully boasting that much of their art and culture predates that of the north, where old traditions were supplanted after the 13th century during the long periods of rule by non–Chinese nationalities such as the Mongols and Manchus. The province's rich cultural heritage is strikingly evident in its thriving craft workshops. Few Chinese crafts have been more highly prized in the West than *blanc–de–Chine*, the fluid and elegant white porcelain produced at Fujian's Dehua kilns. During the last 300 years small Dehua figurines of Buddhas, Guan–yin (the Buddhist Goddess of Mercy), and other legendary beings were extremely popular as export items to the West. The region around Dehua has ample amounts of fine, white clay which is rich in the kaolin necessary for making the finest porcelains. Many of the deities and mythological figures, gracefully molded under a thick, creamy glaze, are still fired in the old way within wood–burning, multi–chambered "dragon kilns."

Partly because of its wealth of fine crafts, textiles, and tea, and partly because of the low agricultural productivity in all but the narrow eastern coastal plains, natives of Fujian turned to maritime trade for a livelihood centuries ago. And over 900 years ago Arab, Syrian and Southeast Asian merchants were steering to the ports of Fuzhou, Quanzhou, and Xiamen to trade their holds full of pearls, spices, and rare woods. Fuzhou's long tradition of commerce and craftsmanship continued after the city was opened to the West by the Treaty of Nanking in 1842, bringing an influx of European merchants and missionaries to settle in the city. Today Fuzhou continues to be the center of a vigorous trade in crafts produced locally and within the province.

What to Look For

Although Fuzhou is not as popular a tourist center as many other Chinese cities, visitors who come here can find a variety of local and regional crafts. Probably most famous are the boxes, vases, tea sets, and trays made of light–weight bodiless lacquer. Screens and traditional furniture made of painted lacquer with inlay of semi–precious stones or mother–of–pearl on a wooden base are also available. Softstone carvings of seals, figurines, and landscapes in relief are popular as well.

The small village of Xiyuan north of Fuzhou specializes in intricate cork mosaics which are sold in Fuzhou along with polished longyan wood carvings. From Dehua come fluid, creamy white porcelains known as *blanc–de–Chine*, which have long been popular in the West and continue to be produced today. Folk arts such as painted oilpaper umbrellas and paper lanterns are another specialty of Fuzhou residents. You may find beautifully painted and carved wooden hand and string puppets with embroidered silk costumes. Fujianese puppeteers have gained an international reputation for their amazing skill and virtuosity in manipulating these figures. And before you leave, you may want to buy some of the rich, semi–fermented oolong teas grown in the Wuyi Mountains northwest of Fuzhou.

Where to Look

The best source for bodiless lacquerware is the retail shop of the Number One Bodiless Lacquerware Factory on Xinping Road. The Fuzhou branch of the Fujian Tourist Souvenirs Production and Supply Corporation on Wusi Road stocks a tremendous variety of local and regional crafts, including stone and wood carvings, lacquerware, porcelain and silk. A walk along the narrow lanes and side streets of the city will take you past many interesting little shops selling painted paper umbrellas, woven bamboo goods, and paper lanterns.

Highly Recommended ★ ★

1. Fuzhou Number One Bodiless Lacquerware Factory Retail Shop ★ ★
16 Xinping Road

第一脱胎漆器厂门市部
新平路16号

Hours: 9–6 daily

Accepts traveler's checks and major credit cards

Has English–speaking staff

Recommended Crafts

• lacquer stacking trays and stacking boxes decorated with traditional designs of flowering plum, pine, or narcissus against a mirror–like black ground
• lacquer reproductions of antique ceramics such as celadon bowls, Tang polychrome glazed horses, and neolithic painted pots.

At Fuzhou's Number One Bodiless Lacquerware Factory visitors can see the lengthy process of hand work which goes into making bodiless lacquerware. These lustrous yet feather–light pieces are formed by building up layer upon layer of lacquer—sometimes over 100 coats. The process was discovered about 200 years ago by Shen Shaoan, a Fuzhou lacquerware maker whose shop was the forerunner of the present Number One Bodiless Lacquerware Factory. Today a visitor is met by the overwhelming odor of liquid lacquer, made from the refined sap of the lac tree that is native to south and central China. The courtyard of the factory is a fantastic moonscape heaped with shards of broken plaster molds that have been used to make the clay bases for the lacquer objects. The secret of the process lies in applying lacquer onto pieces of cloth which cover the clay bases. After the many coats of lacquer have been applied and dried, the clay bases are removed. The result is almost weightless objects. Applying the lacquer is a tricky business. Each coat must dry thoroughly in a moist, temperature–controlled, dust–free atmosphere. After drying, each layer is ground and polished before the next coat is applied, and the final layer is buffed to a mirror–like sheen.

Workers at this factory literally hand polish the black–lacquer screens and inlaid vases, applying a pumice powder and buffing the lacquer surfaces with only their naked palms. The craftsmen explain that this gives them better control over the polishing process and yields a more even and luminous surface. It is no wonder that Fuzhou's bodiless lacquer is called one of China's three craft treasures, ranking alongside the colorful and intricately wrought cloisonné enamel of Beijing and the superb porcelains of the old imperial kilns at Jingdezhen in Jiangxi Province.

The bodiless lacquer of Fuzhou can be shaped with a remarkable resemblance to crafts in other media, including bronzes and ceramics. The master craftsmen at the factory have re–created elegant, pale green celadons and robust, Tang polychrome glazed ceramics in a lacquer medium with such success that the resemblance is belied only when one lifts a piece to find it nearly weightless.

At the retail store attached to the factory, you may select from an extensive range of bodiless lacquer vases, figurines, stacking tray sets, boxes, and wine and tea services. All of these pieces are practical as well as decorative, because their finish makes them color–fast and resistant to breakage, heat, and corrosion. The most extraordinary items here are the lacquer reproductions of antique celadons or vibrant Tang polychrome glazed ceramic horses, which are stunningly similar to the ceramic originals. The factory even makes lacquer reproductions of neolithic pots, with swirling, abstract patterns. You can find a large variety of painted and pearl–inlaid lacquer screens and traditional furniture. Prices range from 15 *yuan* for a painted lacquer box to 10,000 *yuan* for a huge, black lacquer folding screen with mother–of–pearl inlay.

Recommended Stores ★

1. **Fujian Tourist Souvenirs Production and Supply Corporation, Fuzhou Branch ★**
   Wusi Road
   Telephone: 33491

   旅游产品生产供应公司
   五四路

Hours: 9–6 daily

Accepts traveler's checks and credit cards

Has English–speaking staff

Recommended Crafts

- bodiless lacquer trays, boxes, tea sets, and small table screens (15–200 *yuan*)
- landscapes and figurines carved of local Shoushan stone or longyan wood (5–100 *yuan*)
- Dehua porcelain figurines (30 *yuan* and up)

At this shop travelers can find an exceptional variety of local and provincial crafts at very inexpensive prices. In addition to elaborate embroidery and bodiless lacquer, Fuzhou specializes in stone and wood carving. A local type of softstone, called Shoushan stone, is used in carving intricate relief landscapes and genre scenes in miniature. The stone has a fine texture and range of colors, including gray, green, yellow, and red. Local craft workers also excel at carving small figurines and scenes using the wood of the longyan fruit tree. At this shop you will find both types of carving, as well as intricate cork mosaic landscapes carved from the soft bark of the *ruan mu*, or oriental oak tree. Another regional craft to look for here is the fluid white porcelain figures made at Dehua to the southwest.

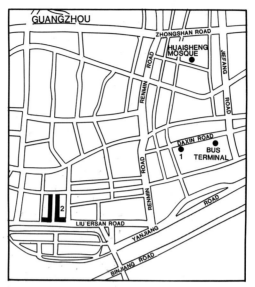

1 Daxin Ivory Carving Factory Retail Shop
2 Qingpin Road Free Market

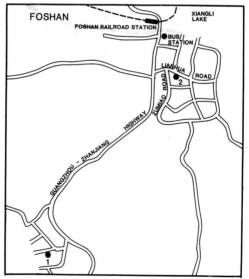

1 Shiwan Artistic Ceramics Factory Retail Shop
2 Foshan Folk Art Research Society Retail Shop

Guangzhou and Foshan

Guangzhou, or Canton, as the city has been commonly known in the West, was the only Chinese city officially opened to Western trade for most of the 18th and 19th centuries. Here, on a narrow strip of land little more than 1,000 feet long on the bank of Shamian Island, foreign traders came to unload their cargoes of rhinoceros horn, spices, ivory, sandalwood, raw cotton, and manufactured goods. They traded these for Chinese tea, ceramics, carved ivory, lacquerware, and silk. Opium from India was, of course, the mainstay of European trade with China in the 19th century, but such contraband cargoes made their way ashore by more circuitous, less public routes.

Arrival in Guangzhou was an unforgettable experience for the traveler new to the East, as we can see from the vivid description provided by a Dr. C. Toogood Downing, who arrived here in 1836.

Many descriptions of the Town of Boats at Canton have been given, but none of them I should think can convey to the reader a distinct idea of the wonderful place, unequalled in singularity by any other spot on the surface of the globe. The crowd of boats of all sizes, shapes, and colours, passing in every direction, with the hubbub and clamour of ten thousand different sounds coming from every quarter and with every variety of intonation, make an impression almost similar to that of awe upon the first visit of the stranger. Upon myself, the excitement produced was so great that I can even now recollect it...After clearing the narrower channels and entering the open stream again, a passage is chosen among the long line of junks which are moored one behind the other, and in rows side by side, in the middle of the stream. These are the vessels which have either just returned from, or are on the point of starting for sea...Some of them are moving off with the tide, all hands on board heaving at the cable to haul up their enormous anchors. The confused noise among them is mixed with the beating of gongs and the firing of vast numbers of crackers which, with the burning of ghost–papers, is the ceremony which always takes place to give the ship a parting farewell, and to appease the spirits of the winds and waters.

Others again are taking in the last of their cargo, and are surrounded by a bevy of small boats. But the generality are lying quietly moored, with their great goggle eyes looking out, apparently, for a change of wind. As you pass along, the Dutch factory is to be seen on the right–hand side of the river. It is some time before you are able to distinguish it beyond the brushwood of spars and masts belonging to the small boats which are crowded together from the shore nearly half–way across the stream. They are of every shape and kind of construction, but are chiefly inhabited by artisans of different trades and occupations, who make these little san–pans their workshops. The noise which arises from this complicated manufactory may well be imagined, and is very similar to that which we hear among the great factories at Birmingham when business is more than usually pressing. (C. Toogood Downing, *The Fan–Qui in China in 1836–7*, reprinted in Shannon, Ireland by the Irish University Press, 1972, Vol. I, pp. 231–4.)

And yet the European traders, restricted as they were to their rented space on Shamian Island, saw almost nothing of China. Very few spoke any Chinese, and they had little conception of the walled city of Guangzhou and the vast empire which lay beyond their factories.

Guangzhou has a long history and a place of importance in the developmentof south China. The city was probably founded in the 3rd century BC as part of the First Qin Emperor's campaign to consolidate the empire. For centuries the city has been a gateway for foreign contacts, receiving numerous foreign residents from Persia, India, and the countries of Southeast Asia from the 8th century on, while the first Europeans arrived from Portugal in the 16th century.

The area has a long tradition of skill in a variety of crafts, foremost being ceramics from the city of Shiwan, located 10 miles southwest of

Guangzhou. Pottery with impressed or painted designs dating from the Neolithic Age has been discovered in Shiwan. By the Tang Dynasty, Shiwan had begun to be established as an important pottery production center. During the Tang an official bureau to oversee foreign trade and control import and export duties was established in Guangzhou, ceramics constituting the majority of items for export. In the centuries that followed, Shiwan ceramics continued to be a major part of Guangzhou's exports. Along with this thriving trade in ceramics, Guangzhou developed a reputation for its intricately–carved ivory. Dr. Downing, quoted above, also marveled at the skill of local carvers in creating spheres within spheres from one piece of ivory.

One kind of article more especially has excited a great deal of interest, on account of the pains which have been taken to discover the way in which they are made. I mean those large balls of ivory cut in a beautiful manner, with from five to fifteen smaller spheres contained one within the other. These appear to be the true Chinese puzzles, which foil the efforts of the Fan–quis [foreign devils] to discover the mode of constructing them. For a long time, it was supposed that there was some joint or other about them, by which they had been fastened together after the balls had been successively inserted; but this idea was quickly banished, when every means had been devised without success to discover where this invisible point of junction was situated. Not to give up the point without trying every thing which offered a chance of success, the ivory globes have been macerated and boiled for a considerable time in water, in hopes that the glue, or whatever cement might have been used, would be dissolved and thus give up its hold. Since this plan has failed, it appears to be perfectly settled that they must be the work of the turning lathe, but of the kind of instruments used for this purpose we have no conception. Many instruments have been made at Birmingham and elsewhere for the purpose of imitating these curious trifles, but with a very indifferent degree of success. (Downing, Vol. 2, pp. 66–8.)

Today the factories on Shamian Island are long vanished. The churches, banks, and foreign government offices which were built in the succeeding years are now schools, apartments, and barracks. Foreign business people now lodge at a newly built 28–floor, five–star luxury hotel, the White Swan, which towers over Shamian Island. They throng to the semi–annual Canton Trade Fair, which in 1985 received 27,000 participants purchasing $3 billion worth of Chinese products. Guangzhou has thus maintained its importance as a gateway for Western contact and as a trade center. The enterprising, ambitious, and earthy outlook which has fuelled the commercial success of its citizens for centuries continues today.

What to Look For

Guangzhou and the nearby towns of Foshan and Shiwan have a long history of skill in ceramics, metalwork, silk weaving and embroidery, enamelware, and ivory carving. In the 19th century European and American traders came to Guangzhou to order porcelains, ivory carvings, and enamelware which local craftsmen had adapted to suit Western tastes. Today's visitor will find good buys in porcelain dinnerware, glazed stoneware figurines, and miniature clay sculptures made in Shiwan. Intricately designed papercut landscapes, paper lanterns, plaster sculptures, and carvings made from cuttlefish bone and ox horn are all specialties of craftsmen in nearby Foshan, and can be purchased in Foshan or Guangzhou. The elaborately–carved wooden panels which decorate temples and old buildings in this region may occasionally be available in craft stores and free markets.

Carved ivory jewelry, figurines, and scenery have long been a specialty of Guangzhou carvers, who continue to devise more and more intricate openwork and miniature details in their sculpture. The embroidery of Guangdong Province, known as "Yue" embroidery, incorporates gold and silver thread with rich shades of red and green in deep relief effects which make the stitchery highly decorative. Seed pearls, semi–precious stones, and threads made from brilliant peacock feathers also embellish this ornate embroidery, used for festive attire, temple hangings, and stage props and costumes.

Where to Look

The Daxin Ivory Factory is located at 415 Daxin Road. The Qingping

Free Market is in the western part of the city on Qingping Road where it intersects Liuersan Road across from the bridge to Shamian Island. Foshan and the neighboring city of Shiwan are about 10 miles southwest of Guangzhou, and are easily accessible by car. The Foshan Folk Arts Research Society is located near the intersection of Zumiao and Lianhua Roads in Foshan, and the Shiwan Artistic Ceramics Factory is on Dongfeng Road in Shiwan, southwest of Foshan.

Highly Recommended ★ ★

1. Shiwan Artistic Ceramics Factory Retail Shop ★ ★
17 Dongfeng Road, Shiwan City
Telephone: 86792

石湾美术陶瓷厂门市部
石湾镇东凤路17号

Hours: 9–6

Accepts traveler's checks and credit cards

Has English–speaking staff

Recommended Crafts

- glazed sculptures of fishermen, little boys riding water buffaloes, and famous figures from Chinese history (20–50 *yuan*)
- miniature scenes of old scholars drinking wine or smoking pipes, for use in miniature potted landscapes (2–5 *yuan*)
- delicate sampans with every detail of mast and rigging re–created in clay (15 *yuan*)

Shiwan has traditionally been called the "pottery capital" of south China, where ceramics have been made for centuries to suit the everyday needs of the people of south China. The flavors of food are said to be enhanced when cooked in pots from Shiwan, and flower pots, vases, and storage jars with brilliant glazes decorate homes and parks throughout China. The kiln center, the largest in south China, is known for its fine crystalline glazes, professional artwork, everyday cookware, industrial porcelain, and small sculptures.

Visitors at the Shiwan Fine Arts Ceramics Factory can see the process of making beautiful glazed stoneware and pottery figurines, boldly modeled and colored with vivid glazes. Original designs for the small figures are produced by the studio's sculptors, and molds are made from these. Fine sculptural details are then added by hand and the figures are polished for a smooth, even look. The figures are then carefully hand painted. Last comes the glazing and firing. The works, although mass produced, receive individual attention from artisans with high professional standards. Traditional subjects include historical and legendary figures, fishermen, peasants, herd boys, and animals. The bold and simple figurines are realistically sculpted and glazed, their facial features emphasized by leaving flesh areas unglazed. The factory also specializes in artistic wares and reproductions of many styles of classical ceramics with a variety of glazes.

In another area of the factory, potters shape tiny figures which decorate *pen–jing*, or miniature potted landscapes with dwarf trees. It is fascinating to see the workers, most of whom are women, rolling thin lengths of dough, impressing careful designs, and then shaping them into tiny scenes such as those of two old men drinking wine or smoking pipes. Also look for the exquisitely fashioned four–inch–clay sampans with thread–thin rigging and delicate sails. The only difficulty with these tiny boats is that they must be very carefully packed or they will snap in transit.

Recommended Stores ★

1. Daxin Ivory Carving Factory Retail Shop ★
415 Daxin Road
Telephone: 822870

大新象牙工艺厂门市部

Recommended Crafts

- ivory necklaces and earrings (100 *yuan* and up)
- figurines and landscapes with elaborately carved details (350 *yuan* and up)

- magnificent ivory carving of Chang E flying down to earth, containing 41 concentric spheres (55,000 *yuan*)

Guangzhou has for several centuries been the center of the southern style of ivory carving, which is generally more elaborate and full of decorative detail than that of the north. Traditional subjects of the Guangzhou ivory carvers include multiple, concentric spheres and ornate, multi–level "flower boats" with detailed human and architectural features. In the 17th century, Guangzhou ivory carvers were so renowned for their superior skill that they were summoned to Beijing by the Kang–xi emperor to work in his palace workshops. These workshops produced amazingly detailed and elaborate landscapes in ivory, often complete with human and animal figures and background filigree designs. Carving concentric spheres, each of which spins freely within the others, has been a special skill of Guangzhou carvers for centuries. Today this is a specialty of the Daxin Ivory Factory where as many as 50 of these concentric spheres have been carved from a single ivory globe.

Visitors to the factory can see the amazing techniques by which these spheres emerge. The process involves drilling diagonal holes to permit the use of a special right–angled tool to carve the spheres, working from the inside to the outside. The artisan can tell if the tool is accurately positioned only by its sound and feel. The last step is to carve the surface of each sphere, working back from the outside to the inside, adding intricate designs to each sphere. Often the spinning balls are part of the total design, as in a stunning modern sculpture of the moon goddess Chang E, who is pictured flying down from the moon, carved in concentric spheres, to visit earth.

Remember that U.S. law prohibits the importation of ivory from whales, walruses, or any source other than the African elephant. Such pieces will be confiscated at the point of entry. You also may bring back African ivory pieces for your personal use, but not in large quantities for commercial purposes. (Commercial transactions require a special permit.) The Indian elephant is classed as an endangered species, and products of Indian ivory cannot be brought into the U.S.

2. Foshan Folk Art Research Society Retail Shop ★
Near intersection of Zumiao and Lianhua Roads, Foshan
Telephone: 86810

佛山民间艺术研究社外宾服务部
佛山在祖庙路和莲花路的交叉口

Hours: 9–6

Accepts traveler's checks and credit cards

Has English–speaking staff

Recommended Crafts

- large papercut pictures of landscapes and farming scenes, painted or unpainted (10–30 *yuan*)
- sets of multicolor floral papercuts (3–5 *yuan*)
- colorful paper lanterns in animal shapes

Visitors to Foshan will enjoy touring the Folk Art Research Society, which is housed in a former temple. Here you can see craft workers producing a Foshan specialty—intricately–cut paper scenes of fields and mountain landscapes. These large scenes are cut so that only the delicate outlines remain, creating a latticework effect. Some pieces are hand painted with vivid colors which, coupled with the cut–paper outlines, create a three–dimensional feeling.

Foshan is also known for its elaborate floral designs cut from multicolored paper and gold or silver foil. Papercut sets showing animals, small children, and famous scenery of China are also popular craft items here, along with elaborate paper lanterns in the shape of dragons, phoenixes, or tigers. Plaster sculptures of animals and human figures and ox horn carvings, traditional specialties of Guangdong Province, are also available here. A new craft of recent years is the carving of cuttlefish bone sculptures which, although intricate, may not be to everyone's taste.

3. Qingping Road Free Market ★
Along Qingping Road near the intersection with Liuersan Road, across from the bridge to Shamian Island

清平路自由市场

清平路在六二三路的交叉口

Hours: variable, but generally open each day until late in the evening

Accepts cash only

No English–speaking vendors

Recommended Crafts

Merchandise will vary considerably depending on the time of your visit, but you may find some of the following:

- reproductions of Ming and Qing Dynasty ceramics, especially blue–and–white underglazed porcelain vases (8 *yuan*) and plates
- blue–and–white ceramic pillows in the shape of reclining baby boys (25 *yuan*)
- gilded and intricately carved wooden panels and figures (30–100 *yuan*)
- teapots in the shape of a duck (3 *yuan*)

Jostling along the narrow lanes off Qingping Road, the visitor to Guangzhou gets a glimpse of old and new China: old because private vendors and outdoor markets have been a basic feature of Chinese economic life for centuries, and new because such free markets have only been reinstated since the early 1980's. The Qingping Free Market is divided into several sections selling vegetables, live fowl and animals, goldfish, birds and bird cages, and antiques and reproductions. To find the latter, you must pass by bamboo baskets and wooden cages displaying turtles, snakes, frogs, monkeys, dogs, and pangolins destined for someone's table. Such animals are sometimes included in the diet of people living in Guangzhou and south China, but are not generally consumed elsewhere in the country. The selection of ceramics is good, especially the reproductions of blue–and–white Ming and Qing Dynasty porcelains. Many of these are seconds, but if you choose carefully and watch for uneven glazing, pitting, and cracks, you should be able to find some nice items at very reasonable prices. Craft items vary considerably, but on a recent visit we saw 18–inch blue–and–white underglazed vases and unusual teapots in the shape of a duck. Blue–and–white ceramic pillows in the shape of baby boys were another unusual item available here, along with traditional gilded wooden panels, seals, and old silver. Vendors also display pieces which are said to be antiques, but it is unlikely that any objects here are more than 50 or 60 years old. Nevertheless, if you like a piece and understand that it is probably not of great age, you may be very pleased with your purchase. Also remember that bargaining is expected.

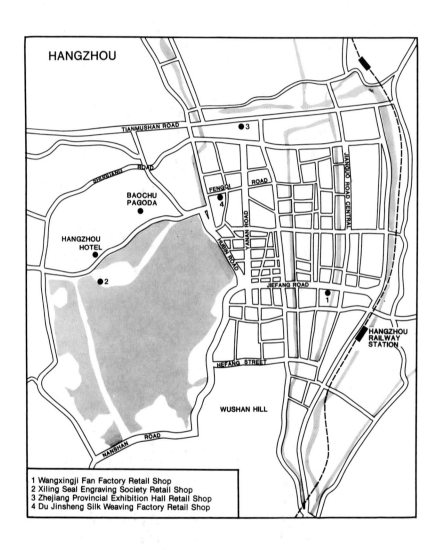

HANGZHOU

TIANMUSHAN ROAD

● 3

SHUGUANG ROAD

FENGQI ROAD

BAOCHU
PAGODA

JIANGUO ROAD CENTRAL

4

HANGZHOU
HOTEL

YANAN ROAD

HUBIN ROAD

● 2

JIEFANG ROAD

1

HANGZHOU
RAILWAY
STATION

HEFANG STREET

WUSHAN HILL

NANSHAN ROAD

1 Wangxingji Fan Factory Retail Shop
2 Xiling Seal Engraving Society Retail Shop
3 Zhejiang Provincial Exhibition Hall Retail Shop
4 Du Jinsheng Silk Weaving Factory Retail Shop

Hangzhou

Whether viewed at first light in a halo of red, gold and purple clouds or lit by a full moon; whether seen in spring when the causeways are swept with green willows and lush flowering peach trees, or on a rainy day when sky and water are joined in mist, Hangzhou's West Lake is a vision of unparalleled beauty rightly termed a paradise on earth. Cradled on the north, west, and south by emerald mountains reflected in the translucent lake waters among a rich tapestry of flowering water lilies, the city has long been famous for the beauty of its scenery and the excellence of its crafts.

By Chinese standards Hangzhou is not an ancient city. The area was formerly a shallow bay in the Qiantang River. Through the combination of alluvial soil deposits carried by the river and man–made dikes, a separate lake was created here. The town grew up on its present site east of the West Lake. The construction of the Grand Canal in the 6th century brought increased trade and economic life to the region. Then, in 1126, the Song imperial court moved south to escape the advance of northern non–Chinese invaders, finally settling upon Hangzhou as their new, provisional capital. This brought the flowering of Hangzhou.

By the 13th century the city had grown to become the most wealthy and populous in the world, with its population exceeding one million. Every kind of luxury could be found here, from rare delicacies, luxurious silks, finely wrought gold and silver jewelry, hair ornaments, and fans to "beauty products (ointments and perfumes, eyebrow–black, false hair), pet cats and fish for feeding them with, "cats–nests," crickets in cages and foodstuff for them, decorative fish, bath wraps, fishing tackle, darts for the game of "narrow neck," chessmen, oiled paper for windows, fumigating powder against mosquitoes..." (Jacques Gernet, *Daily Life in China on the Eve of the Mongol Invasion*, Stanford, California: Stanford University Press, 1962, p. 48)

Under the Southern Song Dynasty, imperial pottery workshops were established in Hangzhou to provide fine pieces for the use of the court. Thickly covered with a glaze of pale blue, gray, or blue–green, with a network of fine cracks, these pieces were dignified by great elegance and restraint. The high degree of organization in their production has been revealed by a recently–excavated imperial ceramic workshop on the outskirts of Hangzhou, where a "dragon kiln" was capable of firing 10,000 pieces at one time.

When Marco Polo travelled to Hangzhou in the 13th century, he marvelled at the wealth and size of this city where every kind of craft was practiced and every kind of luxury sold.

> ...the city was organized in twelve main guilds, one for each craft, not to speak of the many lesser ones. Each of these twelve guilds had 12,000 establishments, that is to say 12,000 workshops, each employing at least ten men and some as many as forty. I do not mean that they were all masters, but men working under the command of masters. All this work is needed because this city supplies many others of the province. As for the merchants, they are so many and so rich and handle such quantities of merchandise that no one could give a true account of the matter; it is so utterly beyond reckoning. And I assure you that the great men and their wives, and all the heads of the workshops of which I have spoken, never soil their hands with work at all, but live a life of as much refinement as if they were kings. And their wives too are most refined and angelic creatures, and so adorned with silks and jewellery that the value of their finery is past compute. (Ronald Latham, trans., *The Travels of Marco Polo*, New York: Penguin Books, 1958, p. 217)

Under the succeeding Ming Dynasty, Hangzhou continued to excel in the production and weaving of silk. Today the city still maintains its importance in the silk industry, producing 100 million meters of silk fabric per year, or 1/5 of the country's total output.

What to Look For

Ever since Marco Polo visited Hangzhou in the 13th century, foreign visitors have rhapsodized over the luxurious silks and fine crafts available in this city. Today it is still a good place to browse for brocade, printed crepe, and raw silk, available at very reasonable prices. The locally–made table linens decorated with lace are also well known. Woven silk tapestries with landscape scenes and portraits continue to be popular as souvenir items, as are the Tianzhu brand chopsticks, sandalwood fans, and Zhang Xiaoquan scissors. The silk parasols decorated with colorful embroidery or painted scenes of the West Lake also make charming and practical souvenirs. Hangzhou is a good place to buy the charming woven–bamboo animals, trays, boxes, and baskets which are produced locally and in Zhejiang province. Other distinctive local products to look for are ceramic reproductions of elegant, pale blue–green Song Dynasty "official wares" which were made for the imperial court when it moved south to Hangzhou in the 12th century. And what better to drink in a celadon cup than Hangzhou's Longjing tea, which tea lovers consider to be without peer.

Where to Look

Many shops and craft factories can be found in downtown Hangzhou near the lake. The Du Jinsheng Silk Weaving Factory is located on Fengqi Road several blocks from the water, and the Zhejiang Provincial Exhibition Hall is several blocks north on Yanan Road. You will also enjoy the beauty of the Xiling Seal Engraving Society on Gushan Island just offshore in the West Lake. The Wangxingji Fan Factory is located on Jiefang Road. Depending on your interest and time, you may want to visit the carpet, lace, parasol, bamboo ware, and embroidery factories found in or near Hangzhou.

Recommended Stores ★

1. Wangxingji Fan Factory ★
77 Jiefang Road

Telephone: 28255

王星记扇厂门市部
解放于77号

Hours: 8 – 4:30

Accepts cash only

Has English–speaking staff

Recommended Crafts

- peacock feather fans with carved ivory frames (200 *yuan*)
- large painted folding fans for wall decoration (200 *yuan*)
- black Hangzhou "tribute fans" (10–40 *yuan*)

Hangzhou has a thousand–year tradition of making beautiful fans from silk or paper attached to ivory, sandalwood, lacquer, or bamboo. At the Wangxingji Fan Factory, skilled workers continue to make a variety of traditional styles, includingspecial black paper fans which were produced to rigid specification and sent to the imperial household as tribute items by local officials during the Qing Dynasty. These beautifully painted fans, which require some 80 steps to complete, have been a specialty of this shop since its founding in 1875. Carved sandalwood fans are another specialty of this factory, which today produces over six million fans per year. The factory also makes one–of–a–kind, decorative pieces such as a large carved ivory fan designed to be used as a screen (1,500 *yuan*). After touring the various workshops, visitors can make purchases at the factory retail shop.

2. **Xiling Seal Engraving Society Retail Shop** ★
Gushan Island
Telephone: 21350

西泠印社外宾服务部
孤山岛

Hours: 9–5:30

Accepts cash only

No English–speaking staff

Recommended Crafts

- seals of veined and patterned stone with carved lions or dragons on the top (starting at 50 *yuan*)
- fine quality artist supplies
- rubbings (3–200 *yuan*)

Set amid bamboo groves at the foot of Gushan (Solitary Hill) on the island of the same name, the Xiling Seal Engraving Society devotes itself to research on ancient Chinese scripts preserved on bronze, stone, and paper. Its members meet twice a year within these beautiful surroundings to share new scholarship and plan exhibitions and publications. Those interested in the history of the Chinese written language and the development of the specialized craft of seal carving will find a visit here particularly fascinating.

The craft of seal carving can be traced back 2,000 years in China. It grew out of the practice of using seals to authenticate letters and official documents. Over the centuries the study of archaic styles of script has drawn the attention of scholars, antiquarians, and artists, both because of its value for historical research and because of its aesthetic interest and application in works of art. Today the society sponsors exhibitions of pieces from its own collection and special shows of seals made by famous craftsmen and painters, as well as calligraphy, paintings, and old rubbings.

The objects on permanent display here include an inscribed stone tablet almost 2,000 years old. Those with a special interest in the subject should stop at the small shop located in the former Mountain and Rain Study. Here you can order seals to be carved with the Chinese transliteration of your name, and you can purchase selected calligraphy practice books, rubbings, seal imprints, and fine quality artist's tools. The seals are especially fine and are carved by experts skilled in ancient styles of script. Expect prices to be high in keeping with this level of skill

3. Zhejiang Provincial Exhibition Hall ★
N. Yanan Road
Telephone: 21901

浙江展览馆外宾服务部
延安北路

Hours: 9–6

Accepts traveler's checks and major credit cards

Has English–speaking staff

Recommended Crafts

- woven bamboo figures and containers (10–60 *yuan*)
- reproductions of Song crackle–glaze celadons (15–50 *yuan*)
- printed silk crepe and raw silk (starting from 3 *yuan*/meter)
- silk parasols with bamboo frames

Browsing in this emporium will give you a glimpse of the many fine crafts which come from the Hangzhou region and Zhejiang Province. The store carries a wide selection of woven–bamboo animals and decorative containers, which are a specialty of Zhejiang. Made of fine, split threads of bamboo woven around a bodiless lacquer base, the figures gain a polished finish with the application of a coat of gleaming lacquer. You may be pleasantly surprised by the cost, which is considerably less than that in department and gift stores in the U.S. Other local specialties are printed silk fabric and machine–made brocade pictures, both of which are available here at very reasonable prices. Also look for nubby raw silk in a rainbow of shades, as well as fine satins.

You may fall in love with a West Lake parasol made of colorful silk decorated with painted scenes of the lake or delicate, embroidered designs. Hangzhou is also well known for lacemaking, and the exhibition hall carries a variety of elegant table linens decorated with fine lace details, a famous product of nearby Xiaoshan. If you missed the Wangxingji Fan Factory, you can find their products here, along with charming clay figurines of characters from the local opera. Another well known Hangzhou specialty sold here is the Tianzhu brand of bamboo chopsticks decorated with caps of pearl, silver, or bone. And look for the distinctive pale blue or blue–green vases, figures, and bowls made in Hangzhou in imitation of Song Dynasty imperial wares.

Before leaving Hangzhou, you may also want to buy the two local items which every Chinese visitor wants to take home: Zhang Xiaoquan scissors and Longjing (Dragon Well) tea. Named for a 17th–century maker of scissors, the Zhang Xiaoquan brand is sharp, durable, and beautifully shaped with wide, curving handles. Longjing tea is a special variety of light, fragrant, green tea which has been produced in this area for 1,000 years. It is prized by tea lovers for its fine, slightly sweet taste and is held to be best when brewed in the pure, underground waters of the Tiger Spring, which is located in Hangzhou.

4. Du Jinsheng Silk Weaving Factory Retail Shop ★
215 Fengqi Road
Telephone: 21103

都锦生丝织厂门市部
凤起路215 号

Hours: 8–5:30

Accepts traveler's checks and major credit cards

Has English–speaking staff

Recommended Crafts

- woven silk tapestries of landscapes or birds and flowers (5–35 *yuan*)
- silk brocade fabric decorated with stylized forms of the Chinese character for longevity (8–16 yuan/meter)

Since 1922 the Du Jinsheng Silk Weaving Factory has designed decorative, machine–made brocade table linens, pillow cases, and bed spreads, as well as distinctive tapestries of landscape scenes, portraits, and traditional paintings. After touring the factory, you can stop at the retail shop, which carries tapestries of traditional subjects as well as modern scenes such as San Francisco's Golden Gate Bridge. The shop also sells popular tapestry portraits of Mao Zedong and Zhou Enlai.

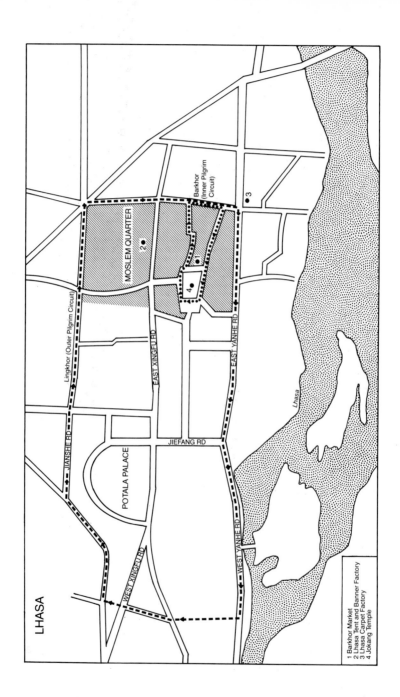

LHASA

POTALA PALACE

MOSLEM QUARTER

Barkhor
(Inner Pilgrim
Circuit)

Lingkhor (Outer Pilgrim Circuit)

EAST XINGFU RD

EAST YANHE RD

JIANSHE RD

JIEFANG RD

WEST XINGFU RD

WEST YANHE RD

Lhasa

1 Barkhor Market
2 Lhasa Tent and Banner Factory
3 Lhasa Carpet Factory
4 Jokang Temple

Lhasa

Girded by the highest mountains on earth, Tibet is a storehouse of ancient religion, art, and social customs. Its attraction for Western travelers remains undimmed since the first missionaries and adventurers dreamed of penetrating the country's secrets. In the early 20th century Lhasa was closed to foreigners, but its forbidden status only enhanced the attraction. The first European woman to enter the sacred city was a French adventurer/mystic named Alexandra David–Neel, who journeyed through Tibet in the guise of a beggar but wisely carried a revolver beneath her ragged robe. After many months she and her young lama guide finally reached Lhasa, just in time to witness the new year celebrations.

A very famous festival takes place each year at Lhasa on the evening of the full moon of the first month. Light wooden structures of a large size are entirely covered with ornaments and images of gods, men, and animals, all made of butter and dyed in different colours. These frail frameworks...are erected along the par kor—that is to say, the streets that form the middle circle of religious circumambulation around the Jo khang, and in front of each one, a large number of butter lamps burn on a small altar. That nocturnal feast is meant to entertain the gods, just as are certain concerts on the roofs of the temples...

As soon as darkness had come and the lamps were lighted, Yongden and I went to the Park Kor. A dense crowd was there, waiting for the Dalai lama, who was to go round to inspect the tormas (butter sculptures)...Groups of sturdy giants, cowmen clad in sheepskin, holding on to one another, ran for joy in the deepest of the throng. Their big fists belaboured the ribs of those whom bad luck had placed in their way. Policemen, armed with long sticks and whips, growing more and more excited as the time of the Dalai lama's coming approached, used their weapons indiscriminately against anybody. In the midst of this tumult, trying our best to guard ourselves against hustling and blows, we spent some lively moments.

At last the arrival of the Lama–King was announced...The knocking, beating, boxing increased. Some women screamed, others laughed...The whole Lhasa garrison was under arms. Infantry and cavalry marched past the dazzling butter edifices, lighted up by thousands of lamps. In a sedan chair covered with yellow brocade, the Dalai lama passed in his turn, attended by the commander–in– chief of the Thibetan army and other high officials. Soldiers marched in the rear. The band struck up an English music–hall tune. Crackers were fired and meagre Bengal lights coloured the procession red and green for a few minutes.

That was all. And the lamaist ruler had gone.

For a long time after the regal cortege had passed, private processions followed: people of rank surrounded by attendants holding Chinese lanterns, high ecclesiastics with clerical followers...nobility, wealthy traders, and their womenfolk all dressed in their best, laughing—all more or less drunk and happy. Their gaiety was contagious. Yongden and I went with the crowd, running, jostling, and pushing like everybody else, enjoying as youngsters might have done the fun of being there in Lhasa, feasting their New Year with the Thibetans." (Alexandra David–Neel, *My Journey to Lhasa*, Boston: Beacon Press, 1986, pp. 269–270.)

The door to Tibet is open today and the road is far smoother than it was for these early adventurers. But the status of tourism to Tibet is still uncertain, as shown by the government response to disturbances in Lhasa at the end of 1987. In November 11987 the Chinese Foreign Ministry announced that Tibet would not receive tourists or visitors for the present time, "except those with the permission of the regional people's government and tourist groups with contracts signed." In reality, tour groups continue to travel to Tibet, and new contracts have already been signed for future tours throughout 1988. Although it is impossible to predict what the future will bring, it is likely that the ban will fall only on individual travel and that group tours will continue to be received. The economic success of opening Tibet to tourism is too remarkable for the policy to be easily changed.

What to Look For

At the outset it is important to note that there has traditionally been little or no secular art in Tibet. On the contrary, the creation of art was considered a religious act to be undertaken only with divine inspiration. Tanka images of Buddhas and mandalas, sculptures, metalwork images, and tapestries—all were produced as guides for meditation, or to pay homage to the Gods.

Today visitors to Lhasa will find few fine examples of religious art available for sale. While Tibetans may offer to sell their own religious objects to travelers, these pieces are seldom of great value, age, or high workmanship. The best available examples of bronze statues or silver amulet boxes are usually purchased by Indian and Nepalese traders and taken to those countries for resale, often at sky–high prices.

The traveler to Lhasa will do better to look for unusual examples of jewelry and costume items such as aprons, shoes, sashes, hats, and robes. Decorative tents and carpets are distinctive and a good value. A great variety of turquoise is also available at reasonable prices.

Where to Look

The best place to look for crafts is along the streets of the old part of Lhasa near the Jokhang Temple, the most sacred of all Tibet's religious sites. Pilgrims still make a ritual circuit of the temple along the octagonal street known as the Barkhor, which is also a busy market area. Here vendors hawk their wares from makeshift stalls or call the merits of carpets and textiles scattered at their feet. Mahogany–skinned Khampa nomads may boldly present their knives or hats for sale, while women laden with pieces of turquoise hanging from strings will offer you your pick. All this negotiation is carried on in cheerful disregard of signs in the Barkhor prohibiting trade or the exchange of money.

As you wander along the tiny, twisting streets of the old city you will also come upon shops selling various crafts and traditional garments, as well as cheap, colorfully printed tankas. Other shops of interest include the Lhasa Tent and Banner Factory, located at the eastern end of Xingfu Road, and the Lhasa Carpet Factory, located on Yanhe Road just east of the intersection with the Lingkhor. If time permits, travelers might also like to visit the Moslem quarter of Lhasa, which is located southeast of the Barkhor. In addition to selling Moslem food, the quarter occasionally offers distinctive items of Moslem dress such as embroidered hats and woven fabric.

Highly Recommended Stores ★ ★

1. The Barkhor Market ★ ★
Located along the Barkhor, the inner pilgrim path around the Jokhang Temple

八角亍市场
大昭寺之附近

Hours: About 9:00 a.m. into the evening, hours not fixed

Cash only No English spoken

Recommended Crafts

- wooden tea bowls with silver lids
- turquoise chunks, veined and unveined (15–60 yuan)
- rosaries with beads of red coral, bone, and turquoise
- long black chuba robes (about 250 yuan)
- ornamental silver daggers

Awaken early and go to the Barkhor just as the fragments of the night give way before the sun's alpine clarity. Smell the pilgrims' clouds of burning incense and fragrant juniper boughs mingling with the ever–present pungency of burning yak dung and yak butter votive candles. Wait for the rising din of commerce along the narrow alleys to blend with the deep murmur of chanted mantras, the flapping of prayer flags and the muffled thump of pilgrims prostrating themselves along this sacred route. When you have experienced all this, you will know that you are in Tibet at last.

Walking along the Barkhor and the narrow alleys that lead away from the Jokhang is like plunging back into time, into a Tibetan way of life little changed by the modern world. Even those with little imagination will feel the pull of history and the power of the deep religious traditions of this region. Buddhist pilgrims have long practiced the clockwise circumambulation of important shrines (*pradaksina*), and this practice continues today along the Barkhor. The circuit approximates the clockwise turning of the Buddhist wheel of the law, and to the initiated represents the progress from ignorance to spiritual illumination.

All along the road are small shops, makeshift stalls, and merchandise scattered along the ground. Leathery–faced old farmers, Khampa tribesmen with high boots and silver daggers, and Nepalese and Indian merchants ply their wares with good– natured aggressiveness. The Barkhor market is characteristically Asian in its fusion of the sacred and the secular.

Do not expect to find exquisite painted or embroidered tankas on silk or fine antique bronze ritual implements. The best are carefully guarded by the Tibetans for their own use or were taken out of the country after the aborted 1959 uprising. With those limitations in mind, it is still possible to discover unusual crafts with strong traditional flavor, and the experience of acquiring them will make them treasured long after you return home.

Most of the crafts found here have some religious function, such as the colorful printed prayer flags, bronze or silver temple bells, rosaries with 108 beads of amber, wood, or coral, and prayer wheels. Especially intricate are the traditional amulet boxes worn by Tibetan women around their necks. Made of silver encrusted with turquoise or coral in intricate patterns reminiscent of the sacred patterns of the Buddhist mandala, the boxes contain scriptures, relics or other tokens that have been blessed by a lama.

Popular secular items for sale include fur hats with long ear flaps, horse bells, copper and silver teapots, silver–studded belts, and silver daggers. Tibetan costumes are colorful and exotic, and may be found here. Look for the long black robe or chuba over which Tibetan women wear colorful aprons woven in horizontal bands of color. Curled–toe Tibetan boots of yak skin with tie–dyed or appliquéd felt are also sold in the market, along with the sheepskin coats necessary to survive the bitter winters.

You may be entranced by the Tibetan jewelry that spills from the women's heads and necks in a profusion of color—turquoise, red coral, ivory, pearls, amber, and crystal set amid silver beads. The women often plait these ornaments within the 108 braids of their hair (a figure symbolizing the number of qualities of an enlightened being) or hang them from large earrings. Turquoise is especially popular for use as rosary beads or decoration on amulet boxes.

Tibetan carpets are another interesting craft to look for here, with small wall hangings or prayer rugs the easiest to locate. Handwoven of wool in bright colors, the rugs are usually decorated with geometric patterns of Chinese influence such as stylized wave borders, thunder pattern meanders, dragons, the endless knot, clouds, and the eight Buddhist symbols. Also look for the small rugs and saddle blankets of pulu, a felt made of moistened yak hair that has been pounded and worked into a heavy fabric,

Foreign visitors can expect to be approached in the Barkhor by Tibetans offering to sell their personal jewelry, daggers, or other items of dress. Haggling is part of the experience, and 50 percent is a fair goal to set in such negotiations. Bargaining is also acceptable at shops, but don't aim to negotiate down more than 25 percent. If you are looking for a special item, the best way to find what you want at a fair price is to go to the Barkhor and compare the merchandise available, ask prices to find the going rate, and then be prepared to bargain. Remember, too, that if there have been a number of tour groups at the market recently, prices may have gone up in response to the demand.

If you decide to buy from an individual, keep in mind that government regulations class any crafts made before 1959 as antiques. Smaller Buddhist religious objects, jewelry and costumes may be freely taken out of China, but in recent years customs inspectors have begun to scrutinize the luggage of people who have visited Tibet during their stay. If a customs inspector feels you have an excessive quantity of old or religious items purchased without red wax seals denoting approval for export, he may choose to confiscate some. Because there is no clear, stated policy on this, travelers are best forewarned.

Recommended Stores ★

1. Lhasa Tent and Banner Factory ★
East Xingfu Road

拉萨帐篷厂
幸福东路

Hours: 9:30–4:30 daily

Cash only

No English–speaking staff

One of the first things one notices in the Tibetan countryside is the beauty of the Tibetan tents. Appliqués with intricate designs of navy or black against a white ground, the tents not only provide shelter and warmth from the ceaseless plateau winds, but reflect with gem–like beauty in the brilliant alpine light. The most popular designs on the heavy cotton tents are geometric motifs of Chinese origin such as the endless knot, the thunder meander, stylized longevity symbols, bats, and dragons. The Tent and Banner Factory will also make awnings or festive canopies to order. Prices run from about 40 yuan for a decorated appliqué canopy to 300 yuan for a large tent. The factory's work is excellent, and the Potala and the Lhasa Hotel number among their clients. The shop may also accept commissions to make traditional robes (chuba) to order. Although conditions here are somewhat primitive, the factory's staff is enthusiastic and eager to be helpful.

2. Lhasa Carpet Factory ★
East Yanhe Road House: 9:00–5:00 daily

拉萨地毯厂
沿河东路

Cash only
No English–speaking staff

The Lhasa Carpet Factory is the largest of its kind in Tibet, containing almost 200 workers. The weaving is done by hand on traditional vertical looms. While the knotting is not as dense as is common in high–

quality Chinese rugs, this looseness is compensated for by the bright colors and deep pile. The rugs have traditionally been used for prayer mats or wall hangings. Geometric patterns continue to be popular, along with the Buddhist swastika, symbol of the perpetuation of the Buddha's teaching for 10,000 years. The eight Buddhist symbols are also a favorite decoration, including the wheel of the law, the conch shell, the lotus, the goldfish, the vase of wisdom, the banner, the endless knot, and the umbrella. The rugs are usually woven in bright colors of red, green, or blue. Prices range from 250 *yuan* for a 1' x 2' carpet to 400 *yuan* for a 3' x 6' size.

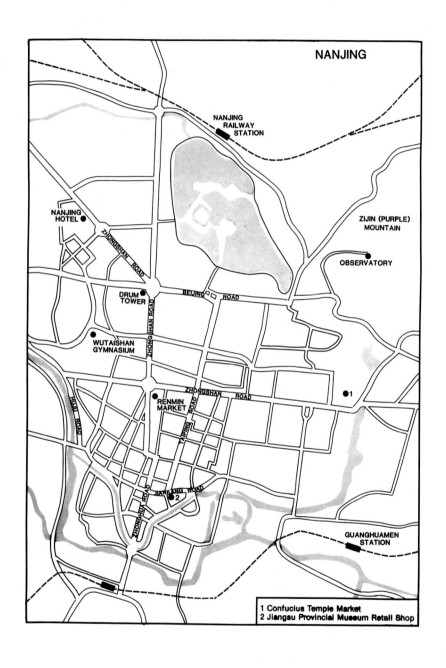

NANJING

NANJING RAILWAY STATION

NANJING HOTEL

ZIJIN (PURPLE) MOUNTAIN

OBSERVATORY

ZHONGSHAN ROAD

DRUM TOWER

BEIJING ROAD

WUTAISHAN GYMNASIUM

ZHONGSHAN ROAD

ZHONGSHAN ROAD

RENMIN MARKET

TAIPING ROAD

HUJU ROAD

ZHONGHUA ROAD

JIANKANG ROAD

●1

●2

GUANGHUAMEN STATION

1 Confucius Temple Market
2 Jiangsu Provincial Museum Retail Shop

Nanjing

Walking through Nanjing, one sees the scattered vestiges of past dynastic glories lying beside startlingly modern landmarks which reveal the face of China's future. Within the green fields around the city, majestic winged stone lions, seated tigers, bold warriors in full battle dress, and tortoises carrying large stelae rise like silent sentinels guarding the memories of the city's past. Their grandeur is now dimmed by the majesty of the awesome Yangzi River Bridge—100,000 tons of steel that span the restless water for almost a mile. Visitors may prefer to survey the city from a revolving restaurant perched at the top of the 37–story Jinling Hotel. But the city's past cultural brilliance and artistic heritage can never be forgotten.

The capital of Jiangsu Province, Nanjing lies protected between the Yangzi on its west and the Zijin (Purple and Gold) Mountains on its east. For centuries this city has been a hotly contested prize, located strategically on the major east–west water transport route provided by the Yangzi. Its history is conveyed by its name, which means "southern capital." The city has been the political center for numerous kingdoms and dynasties beginning with the state of Wu during the Three Kingdoms Period (220–265). In the centuries that followed Nanjing was to become nine more times a capital, twice suffering total devastation at the hands of conquering forces.

Perhaps Nanjing's greatest age came in the 5th and 6th centuries when it was capital for each of the southern kingdoms of Liu Song, Qi, Liang, and Chen. All the splendor and refinement of China's cultural heritage were focused here. Li Yu, the 10th century ruler of the Southern Tang state, whose capital was at Nanjing, was a particular patron of literature, art, and music, and was himself one of China's finest poets. But the city fell before invading Song forces in 975 and the defeated ruler was taken north to the Song capital at present–day Kaifeng. Here he stayed in captivity for three years, writing some of the most moving verses in Chinese poetry.

> Spring blooms, autumn moon, when will they end?
> How many yesterdays have passed?
> Last night, at my little pavilion, the east wind again!
> Oh, lost country, when moon is bright, I can't bear to look back.
> Carved balustrades, marmorean stairs no doubt will stand;
> Only the once bright faces have changed.
> Ask the sum of grief there's to bear,
> It's just a river in full spring flood flowing east to sea.
> (Translated by Eugene Eoyang in Wu–chi Liu and Irving Lo, ed.,
>   *Sunflower Splendor*, Garden, City, New York: Anchor Books,
>   1975, pp. 305–6.)

On his forty–first birthday Li Yu's life of captivity ended when he drank a gift of poisoned wine sent him by the Song emperor. But his poetry describing the lost beauties of his capital at Nanjing still stirs readers centuries later.

> The things of the past may only be lamented,
> They appear before me, hard to brush aside.
> An autumn wind blows in the courtyards and moss invades the
>   steps;
> A row of unrolled beaded screens hangs idly down,
> For now no one comes for all the day.
> My golden sword now lies buried deep,
> And all my youth is turned to weeds.
> In the cool of evening, when the heavens are still and the moon
>   blossoms forth,
> I think of all those towers of jade and marble palaces reflected,
> Shining emptily in the Ch'in–huai.
> (Translated by Daniel Bryant in *Sunflower Splendor*, p. 303.)

In the 14th century, with the establishment of the Ming Dynasty, Nanjing once again came to prominence for a short time. Hong Wu, the first Ming emperor, established his capital at Nanjing in 1368 and ordered a tremendous campaign of construction. The present city walls, the longest in the world, date to this period. A labor force of 200,000 toiled for over 20 years to complete this imposing rampart, which incorporates bricks of the same precise size, each stamped with the name of the brickmaker and the overseer. A majestic imperial palace was also constructed, the forerunner of Beijing's Forbidden City. But the third Ming emperor chose to move the court to Beijing, and the Nanjing palace was allowed to fall into ruin. In the centuries following, fire, age, and successive warfare laid such waste to the magnificent marble halls and glazed roofs that today only a few stone sculptures remain.

Since the 13th century Nanjing has been a key center for brocade production. *Yun–jin*, or cloud–pattern brocade, is the local specialty. According to legend, the skill was taught to local weavers by seven immortal maidens whose job it was to weave the colors of the rainbow and rosy clouds of the evening sky. One day, when the celestial emperor took a nap, the immortals stole away from their labors and came to earth to teach humans their skills. Their patterns resembled the clouds at sunset, giving the brocade its name. Nanjing brocades are distinguished by the quality of the silk threads, some of which are so light and thin as to be almost transparent, making a brocade which is extremely fine and delicate; other brocades are stiff and ornate. Another feature is the high level of skill of the weavers, who may use many different colors of thread in one piece, and in the past even incorporated silver and gold strands and thread made from peacock feathers. Another characteristic is the addition of colorful embroidery to the woven cloth, creating an elaborate, ornate effect. The fabric was very expensive and in great demand for imperial use in court robes and jackets, ceremonial hangings, book covers, and scroll mountings. By the 17th century, Nanjing silk brocades were very popular in foreign markets, too, and widely exported to Japan and Europe.

In the 19th century Nanjing was again the center of turmoil and political struggle. In 1841 during the Opium War the British blockaded China's major ports and sailed up the Yangzi with 10,000 men, prepared to attack Nanjing. And in the following year the first of the "unequal treaties" imposed on China was signed here, opening five ports to foreign trade and ceding Hong Kong to the British. Soon after, the Taiping Rebellion swept across China and the rebel leader Hong Xiuquan established his capital at Nanjing. When the Manchu troops, with foreign assistance, finally recaptured Nanjing in 1864, they destroyed the city.

Throughout these centuries of conflict, Nanjing continued to be an important center for the silk and cotton industries. The city had already become famous for its silk weaving by the 6th century, as well as for its artisans' skill at metalwork and ceramics. During the Ming and Qing Dynasties, weaving became a vast industry. The city had some 50,000 weavers. Despite their skill, working conditions were rather grim. An American traveler who visited Nanjing in the early 20th century recorded her impressions of the exquisite fabrics she saw made there.

> In the ancient capital of China, old looms which have not been improved for centuries can be seen in operation, clattering in the same primitive way that the ancestors worked them. There are no factories as we understand them, but one, two or even six looms will be found tucked away in the farmers' and villagers' mud or cement and stone huts. In these looms are woven the finest gold and silver brocade, stiff with silk and bullion and also the marvellous uncut velvet, produced in designs of lions and elephants, phoenix and dragon, as well as fat gold–scaled fishes and silver pagodas.
>
> One house I visited had a loom in each of the three rooms. The loom was placed directly on the dirt floor with barely enough space to walk around it, while at the back was a narrow *kang* where some member of the family slept during the scant hours allotted for such softer ways of life…A small boy perched on the top of the loom, pulled certain threads rhythmically, while the weaver used many foot treadles to put the threads in position, according to the pattern which seemed to be in his head, as no drawing for a guide was visible. A long metal shuttle carried the gold thread, which was manipulated with skilled accuracy…
>
> More wonderful fabric never was made to gladden the eye of an Eastern potentate. If one is smitten with the desire to possess the gleaming silks so rich with precious metal that they will stand alone, one must seek them in their birthplace in some dark cubby-hole in a weaver's home, or one may sit grandly at home and have Mrs. Wang, or one of her sisters in the trade, call upon you with bundles of delight to be displayed before you and to tempt your pocketbook far beyond your original intention…
>
> Especially I remember one piece of uncut velvet with carp and plum–blossom raised in heavy black pile, so firmly were the fine

threads packed one upon the other and with such superlative evenness; not a blemish marred its smooth perfection of silken sea, wherein the little velvet fishes swam, fat and joyous.

The next day I wended my way through fields of vegetables to Mrs. Wang's home...Arriving at the house I found the usual collection of one–story rooms of uneven dirt floors and stone rooms built to form several courts. In every room was a wilderness of ropes and pulleys of hanging silk–wound bobbins, metal weights and wooden contraptions, with the usual small boy, hanging in midair in the rigging of this extraordinary machine. The whole thing appeared clumsy and grotesquely crude, in its surroundings of dirt and discomfort, yet under the hands of the patient weaver I watched exquisite marvellous beauty come slowly into being. (Grace Thompson Seton, *Chinese Lanterns*, New York: Dodd, Mead and Company, 1924, pp. 318–20.)

What to Look For

Nanjing today produces some 500 traditional craft items. Most famous among its local specialties is the ornate yunjin, or cloud pattern silk brocade, which is woven with multicolor designs of dragons, phoenixes, peonies, and lotuses amid graceful clouds. Nanjing's artisans are also famous for reproducing ancient artifacts such as bronze vessels, wood and ivory carvings, and early glazed pottery. Rubbings made from stone inscriptions and tomb bricks at the many historical sites in and around the city are another important local craft item, as are papercuts.

Chinese visitors to Nanjing always like to take home the colorful agate pebbles from Yuhua (Raining Flowers) Terrace, where legend has it that a 6th century Buddhist monk preached so eloquently that the sky rained flowers which turned into beautifully colored pebbles. The colors of the stones are enhanced in water, making them a popular decoration for fish bowls and miniature landscapes. They are sold at stalls at the Yuhua Terrace and in craft and souvenir stores in the city.

Where to Look

The Confucius Temple is located south of town on the banks of the Qinhuai River. The whole area is presently under development, and renovation should be finished in two years. The Jiangsu Provincial Museum is situated in the eastern part of Nanjing at 321 East Zhongshan Road beside the Zhongshan Gate.

Recommended Stores ★

1. Confucius Temple Market ★
Southern part of Nanjing, by the Qinhuai River

夫子庙市场

夫子庙在太平南路和健康路的交叉口

Hours: Variable

Presently accepts cash only

No English–speakers

Recommended Crafts

- intricately woven palm–fiber brushes with bamboo handles (5–6 *yuan*)
- variety of locally made baskets, which you can see people making on neighboring streets (2 *yuan* and up)

The Confucius Temple has been a busy commercial center in Nanjing for hundreds of years. Today the whole area is being renovated with traditional–style buildings and shops selling local crafts and foods along with areas for evening performances. In the future visitors will be able to buy jewelry, antiques, ceramics, textiles, artist's supplies, and paintings here. Presently there are small shops selling sweets, vegetables, baskets and other local items. An interesting local craft to look for is the beautiful palm–fiber brushes, intricately braided in several layers, made for mounting scrolls.

2. Jiangsu Provincial Museum Retail Shop ★
321 E. Zhongshan Road
Telephone: 41554

江苏省博物馆外宾服务部
中山东路321 号

Hours: 8:30 to 12 noon and 1:30 to 6 p.m.; closed Monday and Wednesday

Accepts cash only

Has English–speaking staff

Recommended Crafts

- reproductions of unglazed Han tomb figures
- reproductions of Tang polychrome glazed figures
- reproductions of painted lacquerware

Housed in a lovely, traditional–style building with red gates and yellow–glazed tiles, the Jiangsu Provincial Museum is the repository of an outstanding collection of artifacts excavated in the province. Displays include ancient bronzes, materials relating to early weaving, tomb figures, Han pottery, Ming and Qing lacquer, jade, ivory and silks. Also in the collection is a Han Dynasty burial suit made entirely of pieces of jade sewn together with silver thread. The museum has a small store which sells antiques and high–quality reproductions. Merchandise varies, but you may find reproductions of unglazed Han tomb figures, Tang polychrome glazed figures, ancient painted lacquerware, or rubbings from the wealth of stelae and tomb sculptures in and around Nanjing.

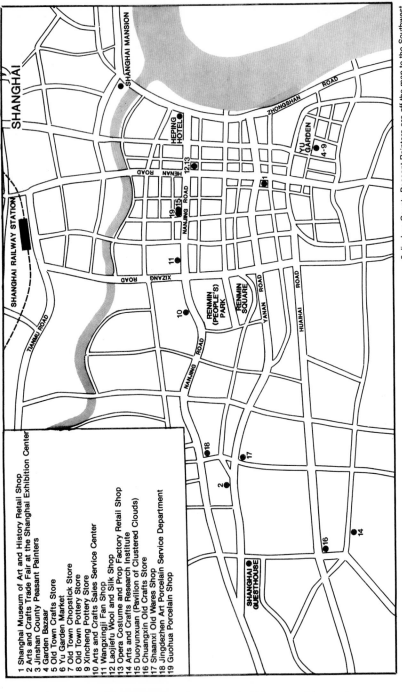

SHANGHAI

SHANGHAI RAILWAY STATION

TIANMU ROAD

SHANGHAI MANSION

HEPING HOTEL

ZHONGSHAN ROAD

YU GARDEN
4-9

HENAN ROAD

12,13

19
15
NANJING ROAD

XIZANG ROAD

11

10

RENMIN (PEOPLE'S) PARK

RENMIN SQUARE

YANAN ROAD

NANJING ROAD

HUAIHAI ROAD

18

2

17

SHANGHAI GUESTHOUSE

16

14

1 Shanghai Museum of Art and History Retail Shop
2 Arts and Crafts Trade Fair at the Shanghai Exhibition Center
3 Jinshan County Peasant Painters
4 Garden Bazaar
5 Old Town Crafts Store
6 Yu Garden Market
7 Old Town Chopstick Store
8 Old Town Pottery Store
9 Xincheng Pottery Store
10 Arts and Crafts Sales Service Center
11 Wanxingji Fan Shop
12 Laojiefu Wool and Silk Shop
13 Opera Costume and Prop Factory Retail Shop
14 Arts and Crafts Research Institute
15 Duoyunxuan (Pavilion of Clustered Clouds)
16 Chuangxin Old Crafts Store
17 Shaanxi Old Wares Shop
18 Jingdezhen Art Porcelain Service Department
19 Guohua Porcelain Shop

3 Jinshan County Peasant Painters are off the map to the Southwest

Shanghai

By Chinese standards Shanghai is a young city, its early development linked to trade in cotton beginning in the 14th century. A native of the city, Huang Daopo, is credited with introducing the skills of spinning and weaving cotton. This eventually led to Shanghai's prominence as the center for manufacture and trade on this textile. During the 17th and 18th centuries, Shanghai continued to develop as a trading and commercial center. But the greatest changes came after the city was forcibly opened to foreign trade by the 1842 treaty which concluded the Opium War. From that point on, Shanghai became the spearhead of foreign presence in China and a base for increasing foreign commercial control. This was the Shanghai of legend and notoriety, the "adventurer's paradise," a glittering cosmopolitan center with unsavory underpinnings.

Commerce, shipping, and business skills have been the city's mainstays for centuries and continue to be so today. Shanghai natives are generally more flexible, outward looking, and up–to–date than other Chinese. They pride themselves on being less hidebound and conservative, and they laugh at the residents of Beijing for being tu or provincial.

What to Look For

Within China, Shanghai is considered a shopper's mecca, the place to come to find the most stylish clothes, the most up–to–date electronic goods, and some of the best arts and crafts. The city's residents are famous for their enterprising spirit, flexibility, and business acumen, all of which add to the pleasure of shopping here. For the foreign visitor,

Shanghai is especially convenient because a surprisingly large number of its salespeople speak good English, and many of its stores can offer a complete range of services such as packing, shipping, and filling special orders.

Shanghai specializes in a number of crafts including embroidery, lacquer inlay, gold and silver filigree work and watercolor wood–block prints, as well as the carving of jade, ivory, bamboo and wood. You can also find a tremendous variety of plain, printed, woven, and embroidered silk fabrics here. Because of the city's important position as an export center, visitors to Shanghai will find key crafts from nearby regions, such as sandalwood fans and double–sided embroidery from Suzhou, painted clay figures from Wuxi, and earthenware teapots from Yixing. You should also look for the city's skillfully painted reproductions of early bronze ritual vessels and animals as well as muted Tang *sancai* ceramic figurines which look as if they have been just unearthed. Among folk crafts, the city is a good source for woven bamboo baskets and bird cages, papercuts, dough figures, hand carved walking sticks, lanterns, and realistic handmade silk and cotton flowers.

Where to Look

Walking past the buildings fronting the waterfront area known as the Bund, a Western visitor in Shanghai feels a peculiar mixture of familiarity and foreignness. Familiarity comes from seeing the many Western–style buildings constructed in this area from around the turn of the century, an unforgettable amalgam of Gothic, Tudor, baroque, ancient Greek, neo–classical, and classic French architecture. The foreignness comes from their setting, which is totally Chinese. This part of Shanghai conveys perhaps the best sense of the city's past—Western architecture from a period of foreign control—and its present—a crowded waterfront busy with the ceaseless activity of freighters and vessels of all sizes carrying the products of China to every country in the world.

The central part of downtown Shanghai, moving west from the waterfront, is laid out in a more or less perpendicular grid of north–south streets named for provinces (such as Fujian, Shanxi, and Henan) and east–west streets named for major cities (such as Nanjing, Beijing,

Hankou, and Fuzhou). The most active shopping areas are found along Nanjing Road, Huaihai Road, and the old Chinese city bounded by Renmin and Zhonghua Roads.

Nanjing Road is the city's most important shopping area, running west from the Bund for over six miles. It crosses twenty–six streets along its length and is most densely packed with stores at the eastern end near the waterfront. Before 1949 this road traversed the center of Shanghai's International Settlement and was a center of modern influences.

> The Shanghainese were inordinately proud of Nanking Road, not only because of its shops overflowing with goods, but because there was truly nothing like it in the rest of China. It was so modern, and nothing enthralled the Shanghainese more than modernity. While the rest of the nation was still sunk in rusticity, here were young girls clacking about on Italian heels, photographic studios, department stores, special offers and seasonal sales, and publicity gimmicks which called for bands to play and even a dwarf got up in a top–hat to cry "Fantastic value! Fantastic value!" outside the shop.
>
> The atmosphere was dictated by the presence of the Big Four— the Wing On (now the Number Ten Department Store), Sincere (currently the Shanghai Clothing Store), Sun Sun (now the Number One Provisions Store), and The Sun (today's Number One Department Store). In their heyday these department stores were more than a collection of shop counters: people came here not only to snap up bargains, but to take tea and cold refreshment, to dine and dance, to listen to oratorios and Shaoxing opera, to skate, to watch comic performances, to look at exhibitions of painting and calligraphy, to play ping–pong and billiards, and to cool down with a pink ice–cream or two. (Pan Ling, *In Search of Old Shanghai*, Hong Kong: Joint Publishing Company, 1983, pp. 58–60.)

Today Nanjing Road houses some 400 stores which specialize in everything from cosmetics, cutlery, fans, and buttons to paintings, opera costumes, medicine, silk and all types of crafts.

Huaihai Road runs east and west in the area which was once the French Concession, south of Nanjing Road and north of the old Chinese city. Formerly called Avenue Joffre, Huaihai Road was the place to go to pass a leisurely afternoon shopping for the new styles from Paris or trading stories with friends at a cafe. Today the eastern and central portions of Huaihai Road house over 200 shops specializing in every type of shoes, clothing, and lingerie.

The Old Chinese City is located in the southern part of Shanghai. As early as the 16th century, walls and a moat were constructed to protect the enclave from the attacks of Japanese pirates who preyed upon China's coast. Today the walls and moat are gone and the circular town is bounded instead by broad Renmin and Zhonghua Roads. But there is still a strong flavor of the past in the narrow, winding streets. Here one comes across the Temple to the City God (Chenghuang Miao), built in homage to an early general, Huo Guang, to solicit his protection for the city.

> The Temple of the City God has been the source of much of the colour and bustle of the city's life, the centre of its festivals and the concourse of its petty trade. Here, too, there were plum–blossom shows in the winter, orchid shows in the spring and chrysanthemum shows in the autumn, where the flowers vied against each other for awards in the "novelty," or "quality" or "rarity" category. Shanghai holds flower shows still, but they are no longer staged in the Chenghuang Miao. Nor are the other familiars—the incense and spirit–money peddlers, the story–tellers and the fortune–tellers— any more in sight, but it is still customary to go to the Chenghuang Miao on Chinese New Year's Day and to gorge oneself on the dumplings traditionally sold in the snack bars outside. The disused temple has had its ceremonial arch, stage and main hall restored to it, while all around it—almost like in the old days—cluster the tea-houses, the sweet shops, the specialist shops and the throngs of Shanghai's teeming populace. (Pan Ling, p. 24.)

Walking farther, one comes to the Yu Garden, a classical southern–style Chinese garden complete with ponds, terraces, galleries, pavilions, fantastically shaped rocks, and narrow paths winding amid pines, bamboo, and willow trees. Located in the heart of the old Chinese city, the garden was constructed in the 16th century by a wealthy official named Pan Yunduan as a private oasis. Today the garden is open to all, and along with the Temple to the City God, has become the hub of a bustling bazaar selling snacks and a wide variety of crafts. It is a fascinating place to wander, to look and be looked at, with one word of advice.

Shanghai has a population exceeding 11 million, and on a holiday it will seem as if they are all congregating here, packed together in jostling unconcern. If you hope to see anything other than the person in front of you, you had better not visit the old city on one of these days.

Highly Recommended Stores ★ ★

1. **Shanghai Museum of Art and History Retail Shop** ★ ★
   16 South Henan Road
   Telephone: 292460

   上海博物馆外宾服务部
   河南南路16号

   Manager: Jin Jiaping

   Hours: 8:30–4:30 (closed afternoons from 11:45–1:00);
   closed Monday

   Accepts cash only

   No English–speaking staff

   Recommended Crafts

   - watercolor albums and landscape paintings copied from pieces in the museum collection
   - reproductions of colorfully glazed Tang Dynasty tomb figures with unglazed heads and faces (100–150 *yuan*); look for a magnificent black charger with minimal use of glaze
   - red–and–black painted lacquerware trays, boxes and cups (40–150 *yuan*)
   - reproductions of pre–Tang painted tomb figures
   - elegant, white–glazed ceramic figures, such as a court musician for 250 *yuan*

   The collection in this museum spans the total range of China's rich cultural history, from 3,000 year–old proto–porcelain and bronze ritual vessels to contemporary examples of cloisonné, lacquer, and embroidery. The exhibits are beautifully displayed, housed in climate–controlled cases, and labeled with background information in clear English. If you can visit only one museum in China, then it should be this one. After viewing this dazzling array of China's cultural riches, forever out of reach to all but the wealthiest collectors, you can fulfill the desire to take some of this beauty home by a stop at the museum's second floor retail shop. This is the place to buy that gift for the person with exquisite taste who already has everything.

The small, rather unprepossessing retail shop features exquisite, specially commissioned reproductions of outstanding original pieces in the museum's own collection. Authentic–looking monochrome landscape paintings on silk, small watercolor albums, and fluid calligraphy are available here at prices which reflect the detail and skillful technique of the copyists. In an adjoining case, patinaed bronze reproductions of small ritual tripod cauldrons and stylized animal figures look as if they have just been lifted from the earth. You may also be lucky enough to come across some exceptional examples of Warring States and Han Dynasty red–and–black lacquerware painted with graceful designs of fighting dragons, dancing birds and mythical animals dissolving into the pure energy of abstract spirals. These elegant trays, cups, and boxes make practical gifts, as well, because the lacquering process gives them a protective layer that permits daily use.

Perhaps the most exciting reproductions in the shop are its carefully chosen ceramics. The museum only commissions a limited number of pieces for display in the shop, so selection many vary greatly, but you can be certain that the objects here have been made with great care, concern for detail, and faithfulness to the original. On past trips I have found reproductions of fierce earth deities that were buried in royal tombs to guard the occupants, as well as imposing Tang multicolor glazed horses in an unusually large size. Look for a black charger with colored glaze limited to the saddle. Captured in a posture of arched neck and down-turned head, the animal is a perfect representation of restrained power and exquisite control. Equally distinctive are the human funerary figures from various dynasties which the museum has commissioned. Colorfully glazed figures of seated musicians and ladies–in–waiting with unglazed faces recreate the vigor of the Tang Dynasty originals.

A completely different feeling is displayed by a strikingly beautiful white glazed figure of a 6th century court lady in a long gown with fluid folds. Plucking her rounded lute–like instrument known as a *pipa*, she seems the very epitome of feminine grace. You may also find Yaozhou celadons with incised designs of flowers or dragons under a thick, glossy green glaze.

The final touch to any of these purchases is their beautiful packaging, a concept which is still rather undeveloped in China. They come nestled in brocade boxes with traditional closings and colorful silk lining. In addition, they carry a red wax seal which verifies that they are reproductions from the Shanghai Museum. These seals are not purely for decoration, but are necessary because the reproductions are so faithful to the originals. In 1984 a hotel worker in Guangzhou grew very suspicious when he saw one of our purchases—the ceramic court lady described above. When he discovered the wax seal, however, he began to smile and confessed that he had been about to report us for trying to smuggle out archeological relics.

Visitors to the Shanghai Museum often find that they cannot view the whole collection in the time allotted. If you are travelling with a tour group, it may be wise to inquire exactly how long you will have in the museum. Set aside a part of that time to visit the retail shop. In its small space are art objects which you will probably never see anywhere else in China.

2. Shanghai Arts and Crafts Trade Fair at the Shanghai Exhibition Center ★ ★
1000 Yanan Road Central
Telephone: 533918

上海工艺展销会
延安中路1000号

Hours: 8:30–11:00 a.m. and 1:00–5:00 p.m., closed Monday

Accepts traveler's checks and all major credit cards

Has English–speaking staff

Recommended Crafts

- unglazed Han Dynasty tomb figures (15 *yuan*)
- black glazed teapot with "oil spot" design, from Boshan (30 *yuan*)
- colorful Guangxi stoneware folk toys (2–10 *yuan*)
- Jinshan County peasant paintings (200–250 *yuan*)

- southern style wood–block print door gods and old farming calendars (5 *yuan*)

Built in the monumental Soviet style of architecture with arched ceilings and towering central spire, the Shanghai Exhibition Center houses permanent exhibitions of over 5,000 of the city's products, from heavy industry and telecommunication devices to watches and toys. The exhibition center was built in 1955 as a "Palace of Sino–Soviet Friendship," but today its cavernous interiors resound to the footsteps of tourists from all countries brought here as part of their Shanghai itinerary.

In the complex there are two crafts shops run by the Shanghai Arts and Crafts Trading Corporation. One is very reminiscent of a Friendship Store. The other, in the left wing, has a fine selection of crafts from all over China. Here you can find not only a vast assortment of every kind of contemporary ware from cloisonné and lacquer to jade and ivory carving, but you can also discover some exceptional examples of folk toys, local ceramics, minority textiles, and peasant paintings, many of which you might not be able to buy even in their own region. An additional attraction here is the sales force. Young, bright, and energetic, the salespeople speak good English and are fairly knowledgeable about the pieces they sell. And if they don't have an answer to your question, they will go and try to get one.

If you missed Rongbaozhai in Beijing you may wish to choose from the wide selection of artist's supplies found here. There are fine reproductions of 2,000 year–old red–and–black painted lacquerware, as well. There are also small, fluid wood carvings of crouching tigers which show the influence of early clay tomb figures, and delicate bowls of "eggshell" porcelain from the Jingdezhen kilns in Jiangxi Province. With walls shaved so fine that painted designs can be seen from either side, these fine porcelains cost hundreds of dollars apiece.

The shop has a carefully chosen array of folk art from many regions of China. The staff who selects these objects has a wonderful eye for form and tradition and seems to come up with exceptional examples of local workmanship. There are colorful, southern style wood–block prints of door gods and old farming calendars as well as the eye–catching gouache paintings of peasant artists from Shanghai's rural county of Jinshan. On one occasion, I found brightly painted stoneware folk toys of animals and fish from Guangxi Province here, which I could not find in the stores of their own region. Another time I saw elegant teapots, from the old ceramic center of Boshan in Shandong Province, decorated in a classical style of glossy black glaze with "oil spot" designs. Although there is only a limited number of these folk pieces and the selection will vary, you will certainly find something special here.

Perhaps the most exciting pieces we have seen on past visits have been the large, painted, stoneware reproductions of Han tomb figures. A court lady with long flowing sleeves and graceful robe with a trailing skirt is startlingly faithful to the Han Dynasty original, but will cost you only 15 *yuan*, one of the best buys in China.

Because of its vast selection, its distinctive folk wares, and its ceramic reproductions, as well as the helpful staff, I highly recommend a visit to this branch of the Shanghai Arts and Crafts Trade Fair at the Shanghai Exhibition Center.

3. Jinshan (Gold Mountain) County Peasant Painters ★ ★
Jinshan County Cultural Center, in rural Shanghai
Telephone: inquire through the Shanghai long distance operator

金山县农民画家
上海郊区，金山县文化管

Responsible Person: Wu Tongzhang, Director of the
Jinshan County Cultural Center

No English–speaking staff

Recommended Crafts

Jinshan peasant paintings are sold unframed from 200 to 300 *yuan*, depending on the artist and size of the piece. The paintings have been sold internationally at considerably higher prices. The artists average about 20 days to complete a picture, as they work only in their spare time. Each artist may paint the same picture many times, each time making slight changes in color and composition. Although all of the paintings are striking, some of my favorites are listed below:

• fanciful paintings of figures from Chinese folk tales and local opera by Chen Dehua

- plump, multicolored ducks and chickens by "Duck Commander" Chen Muyun
- Cao Jinying's blue and white fish pond
- vivid kitchen scenes by Zhang Xinying

For centuries Chinese farming families have used needle, knife and scissors to bring color and beauty to their homes. Their images took shape as wood–block prints, papercuts, embroidery, and weavings which decorated shoes, clothes, chests, beds, and other practical everyday objects. From mother to daughter and father to son the images were passed down for generations. Skill at embroidery was especially valued for women because, as a saying goes, "a woman who cannot embroider will not find a husband." Today these traditional folk skills find exuberant and colorful expression in the paintings of amateur peasant artists of Shanghai's rural county of Jinshan.

Located in the southwest corner of greater Shanghai, Jinshan County seems light years away from the crowds and noise of the big city. The fertile soil south of the Yangzi River is crisscrossed here and there by small streams with arched bridges. Everywhere there is a profusion of color, of golden rapeseed and white flowering cotton against lush green rice fields. In these rich surroundings has developed a colorful folk tradition of indigo and white stencil fabrics, papercuts, lanterns, and elaborately painted beds and wedding chests. The kitchens of Jinshan are especially vivid, as their large ovens of clay and brick are decorated with bright geometric patterns and farming scenes. All of these elements come to life in the gouache paintings of the county's amateur artists. Black fish swirl against white water and red boats of a commune fish pond. White goats wander happily amid mountains of purple, green and blue dotted with flowering trees, while bold red and black roosters march between geometric borders of crisp bamboo plants.

Although peasant painters also work in other regions of China, few seem to have retained the fresh flavor of their folk sources as well as the Jinshan painters have. This is due in no small part to the efforts of the director of the county cultural center, Wu Tongzhang, who feels that the intrinsic folk style of the artists should not be tampered with. The result is a style of folk art which is bold, fresh, and strikingly original. The land and its seasons are the heart of these paintings, and if you fall under the spell of them as I did, then a visit to the commune will add new depth to your appreciation.

The impetus for this art grew out of a 1972 drive to collect and research local forms of folk art. Wu Tongzhang and others from the cultural center traveled throughout the county collecting the exquisitely embroidered aprons, pillow cases, and children's shoes and caps for which the area is known. Women with skills in design and composition became the heart of the project when Wu persuaded them to translate their embroidered images onto paper. Yuan Siti, 74 year–old who has worked embroidery since she was 13, is the eldest of the county's 300 painters, most of whom are women. Her rich colors and vibrant flowers show the clearest influence of an embroidery background. Cao Jinying, 45, uses the patterns of traditional indigo–and–white stencil print fabric to show her two children feeding fat carp which leap from a pond thick with lily pads and all manner of water plants. Chen Muyun, also known as the "Duck Commander," delights in painting plump ducks and chickens in extravagant shades. With their bold colors, geometric patterns, and exuberant style of expression, the Jinshan painters seem to contradict every principle of Chinese painting. But a further look reveals the folk traditions which have nourished and inspired the country's art from earliest times.

Jinshan paintings can sometimes be found for sale in a few Shanghai outlets, such as the crafts shop at the Shanghai Exhibition Center. But if you really enjoy this unique style of art, you will want to schedule a visit to the commune itself, however. It is a two or three–hour trip by car and will require prior arrangement.

4. Yu Garden Bazaar ★ ★
119 Yu Yuan (Garden) Road
Telephone: 289850 (central number)

豫园市场
豫园路119 号

Hours: shops are usually open at least from 8:30 to 5:30

Cash only

No English–speaking staff

Recommended Crafts

- local daily–use ceramics such as food jars and cooking pots

- Yixing teapots
- hand–carved wooden walking sticks
- woven bamboo trays and baskets

Located in the narrow, crowded streets of Shanghai's old city, the Yu Garden Bazaar is a conglomeration of over 100 stalls and small shops which sell all manner of food, clothing, daily–use utensils, traditional crafts and, increasingly, souvenir items. Here visitors can get a feel for the arrangement of an old Chinese city with its labyrinth of cramped, twisting lanes and alleys. As you make your way along the streets you can sample some of the local delicacies: sweet pear treacle, dumplings shaped like pigeon eggs, eyebrow–shaped shortcakes, and five–spice beans. Don't worry if you lose your way—there are bound to be some local English–speakers who will be delighted to conduct you back to a main thoroughfare.

The Yu Garden dates to the 16th century and is a classically styled garden with winding paths, lotus ponds, strangely shaped rocks, and pavillions for viewing different corners of the garden. There is still an air of the past in the neighboring crooked streets, where Shanghai's first missionaries came to establish their churches in the 1800's amid disease–infested slums. Foreigners were then warned not to enter this area without a Chinese escort.

Today a visitor to the shops and stalls of the Yu Garden Bazaar and the nearby Temple to the City Gods (Chenghuang Miao) will not only be rewarded with a glimpse of the pace and daily life of the city, but will also see an array of traditional crafts and daily use items. The colorful wood and paper lanterns are well known, as are the local ceramics such as roughly painted brown and cream ginger jars and cooking pots. You will see all manner of carved and woven bamboo wares, including some whimsically elaborate bird cages. The Wanli Walking Stick Store here specializes in hand–carved wooden walking sticks fashioned with traditional designs such as flowering plum, gnarled pine, or jointed bamboo. On some, coiling dragons writhe up the length of the stick and come to rest at the top to form a handle. Look for a wide range of woods, from bamboo, mahogany, and local red woods to lacquer and metal. Even if you have no need for a walking stick, you may find yourself buying several because of their beauty.

The old town is located in southern Shanghai in a circular area bounded by Zhonghua and Renmin Roads. You will find the Yu Garden

Bazaar in the northeastern part of this district along with a number of shops and stalls clustered by the nearby Temple to the City God. In addition to visiting crafts and food stalls, you may want to stop at some of the shops listed below:

Old Town Crafts Store
1 Yicheng Road
Telephone: 284209
老城隍庙工艺品商店
邑城路1 号

has a fairly standard selection of cloisonné, porcelain, woodcarvings, etc.

Yu Garden Market
6 Yicheng Road
Telephone: 289850
豫园商场
邑城路6 号

Old Town Chopsticks Store
12 Sanlin Road
Telephone: 281012
老城筷子商店
三林路12号

has a variety of inexpensive chopsticks—carved, painted or lacquered

Xincheng Pottery Store
24 Yicheng Road
Telephone: 289850 ext.97
新城陶瓷商店
邑城路24号

has local ceramics, cooking pots, and Yixing teapots

Old Town Pottery Store
60 Yu Yuan Road
Telephone: 289850,
ext. 99 and 265083

老城陶瓷商店
豫园路60号

fascinating shop that specializes in Yixing "purple sand"
unglazed ceramics—special teapots, tea sets, various animals
and figurines

Recommended Stores ★

1. Shanghai Arts and Crafts Sales Service Center ★
190–208 West Nanjing Road
Telephone: 584299 and 581196

工艺美术品服务部
南京西路190-208 号

Hours: 9–9 daily

Accepts traveler's checks and major credit cards

Has English–speaking staff

Recommended Crafts

- finished silk garments
- relief–carved snuff bottles
- shadow figures
- batik fabric from Guizhou

Located on bustling Nanjing Road, the Shanghai Arts and Crafts
Sales Service Center carries a broad range of Chinese crafts, most of
which are produced in Shanghai. There is a particularly good selection
of carvings, including small figures of animals and characters from
Chinese legends sculpted in boxwood, longan wood, bamboo, soft *dong*
and *qingtian* stone, ivory, and jade. The store also has fine double–sided

embroidery from Suzhou, softly shaded Hunan embroideries, and color-ful brocades made locally. Finished silk garments and silk wadding for use as padding are also available, along with papercuts, painted or re-lief–carved snuff bottles, sandalwood fans, shadow figures from Shaanxi Province, and batik fabric from Guizhou Province. Prices run from 2 *yuan* for a set of papercuts to 5,000 *yuan* for carved jade ritual vessels.

2. Wangxingji Fan Shop ★
782 East Nanjing Road
Telephone: 224684

王星记扇庄
南京东路782 号

Manager: Chen Yanlin

Hours: 8:30–8

Accepts traveler's checks but no credit cards

No English–speaking staff

Recommended Crafts

• painted black paper fans
• painted silk fans on carved sandalwood ribs (100 *yuan* and up)
• carved sandalwood fans (32 *yuan*)

For centuries fans have been an essential element of Chinese com-fort and costume. In the heat of summer a round silk fan created a much needed draft as well as a graceful mien, while a folding fan emphasized important points during a conversation. Women carried their delicate fans concealed within a sleeve; men kept their's beneath the back of the collar. Flat fans of silk or soft *xuan* paper decorated with embroidery or painting continue to be popular, as are folding fans made of sandalwood, ivory, lacquer, or bamboo ribs (called "fan bones"). Suzhou and Hangzhou have traditionally been considered the cities that make the best fans in the country, those with ribs intricately carved of sandalwood or of highly polished ivory. Ribs of naturally patterned bamboo, such as "tear drop" bamboo or "phoenix eye" bamboo, are also been much in demand.

The Wangxingji Fan Factory is generally considered to have the best fans in China. Its products run the full spectrum from feather fans for several *yuan* to screens in the shape of carved ivory fans for 1,500 *yuan*. The store also has unusual black paper fans with painted landscape scenes, as well as carved sandalwood fans for 32 *yuan*. Look for exquisitely painted double–sided silk folding fans on carved sandalwood ribs for 100 *yuan* and up and elegant ivory–ribbed peacock feather fans for 200 *yuan*.

3. Laojiefu Wool and Silk Shop ★
257 East Nanjing Road
Telephone: 219292

老介福呢绒绸缎商店
南京东路257 号

Manager: Dong Mingren

Hours: 9–6:30

Accepts traveler's checks and credit cards

No English–speaking staff

Recommended Crafts

- almost any type of silk fabric, including pongee, tussah, crepe
- completed silk garments
- pure silk (9 *yuan*/meter)

A trip to the hundred–year old Laojiefu Wool and Silk Shop is always a crowded business, but the experience of a bustling clientele going through the 1,500 different types of fabric is part of the fun of a visit here. This is the largest silk store in Shanghai and, according to some, in all China.

The store was founded in 1860 and did so well over the years that its owners were nicknamed the gods of longevity and good luck, giving the store its present name of "Longevity Added to Prosperity." In the 1930's much of the store's clientele was foreign, partly due to the store's enterprising salesmen who would go aboard newly arrived ships to solicit customers. It is said that when Charlie Chaplin visited Shanghai he ordered 60 silk shirts in one visit.

A secret of Laojiefu's success has always been the courtesy of its salespeople. The customer truly comes first here. In earlier years clients were invited inside by doormen, and then offerred tea and a choice of pipe or cigarettes. Only after all these formalities had been completed were silks brought out for selection.

Today you can find every color and weight of pongee, tussah, crepe, shantung, damask, satin, and embroidered silk at Laojiefu. The store also carries a limited selection of completed silk garments.

4. Shanghai Opera Costume and Prop Factory Retail Shop ★

259 East Nanjing Road
(Note: The opera store has a display window on the first floor, but another retail store occupies the store space there. The opera shop itself is located on the second floor.)
Telephone: 222640

戏剧服装用品厂门市部
南京东路259 号

Manager: Ji Xinghai

Hours: 8:30–5:30 daily

Accepts cash only

No English–speaking staff

Recommended Crafts

- embroidered Moslem cap (5 *yuan*)
- black silk boots (9 *yuan*)
- embroidered round–toe slippers (17 *yuan*)
- embroidered wedding dresses (150 *yuan* and up)

Because of the great changes in Chinese society during the 20th century, few people still wear the traditional dress in China. Travelers who want to find traditional garments such as robes, tunics and hats have two possible sources: antique shops and opera costume shops. The latter are important for their range of items and their preservation of the costume tradition. Thus a visit to an opera costume shop can be a fascinating experience.

The Shanghai Opera Costume Retail Shop offers an excellent array of clothing, shoes, hats and jewelry based upon earlier historical styles as preserved in Shanghai opera. Although the costumes do not incorporate real gold or silver thread or precious stones, they are intricately worked and authentic in look. In addition to opera troupes, the factory does a brisk business tailoring costumes for martial arts and acrobatic troupes.

Here you can find elaborate opera costume wedding headdresses and colorfully embroidered wedding dresses, as well as pastel silk gowns with floral embroidery for young maidens and scholars. You can also select hats that might be worn in a scholar, magistrate, or general's role, or an embroidered Moslem cap. Some of the most interesting items here are shoes, including black silk boots and elaborately embroidered round–toe slippers. Few items are on display, but salespeople are happy to bring out requested items. If you have time, the store can also make complete costumes to order.

5. Shanghai Arts and Crafts Research Institute ★
79 Fenyang Road
Telephone: 373170

工艺美术研究所外宾服务部
汾阳路79号

Hours: 8:30–5:30 daily (sometimes closes for lunch, however)

Accepts traveler's checks and credit cards

Has English–speaking staff

Recommended Crafts

- dough figures
- papercuts
- needlepoint portraits
- wool carpets (4,500 *yuan*)

Established in 1956, the Shanghai Arts and Crafts Research Institute is housed in a beautiful old European–style mansion, which before 1949 was the home of a wealthy French industrialist. Today a faculty of 160 skilled craftspeople works here to create fine pieces such as realistic portraits and landscapes worked in needlepoint, lanterns, dough figures, papercuts, woodcarvings, inlaid lacquer screens and silk embroidery. While the shop near the ground floor entrance sells the crafts produced here, the main attraction is to see some of China's most skilled artisans at work. A tour and demonstrations may be arranged in advance and are very worthwhile.

Here you can see designers at work making prototypes of the crafts which will later be produced in factories throughout the region. You can watch deft embroiderers split a silk thread into eight strands, each so tiny that it is nearly invisible, and then embroider an intricate floral pattern. In another room skilled artists create amazingly exact copies of European masterpieces, such as the Mona Lisa, in silk or wool needle-point. In 1984 the workshop made a needlepoint portrait based on a photograph of Mrs. Reagan, and the piece was presented as a state gift to Mr. and Mrs. Reagan during their visit to China.

In other rooms you can see elaborate lanterns of dragons, cranes, and lions fashioned in colorful silk and paper, as well as demonstrations of freehand papercutting and dough–figure sculpture. Probably the most astounding craft workers are the carvers who cut complete poems and landscape scenes with miniscule strokes onto a tiny rice–grain size piece of ivory, the finished work so small that it can only be seen with the aid of a magnifying glass.

The Shanghai Arts and Crafts Research Institute was the first insti-tute of its kind to be established in China. With its breadth of specialties and fascinating demonstrations of craft techniques, the institute is well worth a visit.

6. Duoyunxuan (Pavilion of Clustered Clouds) ★
422 East Nanjing Road
Telephone: 223410

朵云轩
南京东路422 号

Hours: 9–5:30

Accepts traveler's checks but no credit cards

Has English–speaking staff

Recommended Crafts

- watercolor wood–block prints (20–200 *yuan*)
- New Year prints from Taohuawu
- wood carvings (300–2,500 *yuan*)
- fans (3–10 *yuan*)

Like Rongbaozhai in Beijing, Duoyunxuan specializes in water-color wood–block print reproductions. Since its establishment in 1900, the store has dealt in calligraphy, paintings, prints, art supplies, fans and seals. Here you can find "the four treasures of the artist's studio"—brush, paper, ink, and inkstone—as well as rubbings from many regions of China. The store also sells fine wood carvings and colorful New Year prints from nearby Suzhou. If you missed Rongbaozhai in Beijing, you can still find an excellent selection of watercolor wood–block prints of China's modern masters here at Duoyunxuan. The store accepts orders to carve seals and mount paintings and calligraphy. An added attraction of a visit is the store's interesting traditional architecture with wooden details and enclosed wooden second floor gallery.

7. Chuangxin Old Crafts Store ★
1297–1305 Huaihai Road Central
Telephone: 372559

创新旧工艺品商店
淮海中路1297-1305 号

Manager: Wei Keqin

Hours: 9–6

Accepts cash only

Has English–speaking staff

Recommended Crafts

- blue–and–white underglazed porcelain brush jars (20 *yuan*)
- carved Buddha of bamboo (40 *yuan*)
- old ivory snuff bottles (400 *yuan*)

If you are looking for an engrossing jumble of secondhand nick-nacks, curios, and old crafts, Shanghai has several commission shops which are worth visiting. Like Beijing's Huaxia, the Chuangxin Old Crafts Store carries an unusual array of old lacquerware, copper and pewter objects, old jewelry, antique ceramics, and old mahogany furniture. You may find blue–and–white underglazed porcelain brush jars, a small carved Buddha of bamboo, old ivory snuff bottles, or an embroidered traditional silk wedding dress (600 *yuan*.)

8. Shaanxi Old Wares Shop ★
557 Yanan Road Central
Telephone: 565489

陕西旧货商店
延安中路557 号

Manager: Yang Qiwen

Hours: 9–6

Accepts cash only

Has English–speaking staff

Recommended Crafts

- small mahogany carvings of animals or Buddhist figures (40–100 *yuan*)
- traditional Manchu *qipao* (60–200 *yuan*)

Like the Chuangxin, the Shaanxi Old Wares Shop sells an eclectic collection of old clocks, watches, bronzes, Chinese and European ceramics, and old jewelry. You may find small mahogany carvings of animals or Buddhist figures, bronze bells or animals, and fine old bamboo baskets (100 to 300 *yuan*). Also look for traditional Manchu close–fitting dresses (*qipao*) and colorfully embroidered silk opera skirts (100 to 300 *yuan*.)

9. Shanghai Jingdezhen Art Porcelain Service Department ★
1175 West Nanjing Road
Telephone: 530885

景德镇艺术瓷器服务部
南京西路1175 号

Manager: Hu Songping

Hours: 9–8

Accepts traveler's checks and credit cards

Has English–speaking staff

Jingdezhen's fine porcelains have been called "white as jade, light as glass, thin as paper, and resonant as chimes." Visitors to Shanghai will find a wide selection of these wares at the Jingdezhen Art Porcelain Service Department. Here you can find exquisitely thin "eggshell" cups and bowls, complete dinner services decorated with blue–and–white floral designs, landscape scenes, or dragon motifs. The store also carries lamps constructed with porcelain bases. If you need to locate individual pieces to complete place settings, the store can also supply them.

10. Guohua Porcelain Shop ★
550 East Nanjing Road
Telephone: 224526

国华瓷器商店
南京东路550 号

Hours: 9–6

Accepts traveler's checks and credit cards

Has English–speaking staff

The Guohua Porcelain Shop specializes in Jingdezhen porcelain and offers a wide range of services to its customers. Here you can select a complete set of blue–and–white or vibrant *famille rose* porcelain, then have it packed and shipped directly home. The store also has a mail order department, and its own studio which can repair old porcelains or take orders to create new, individually painted pieces.

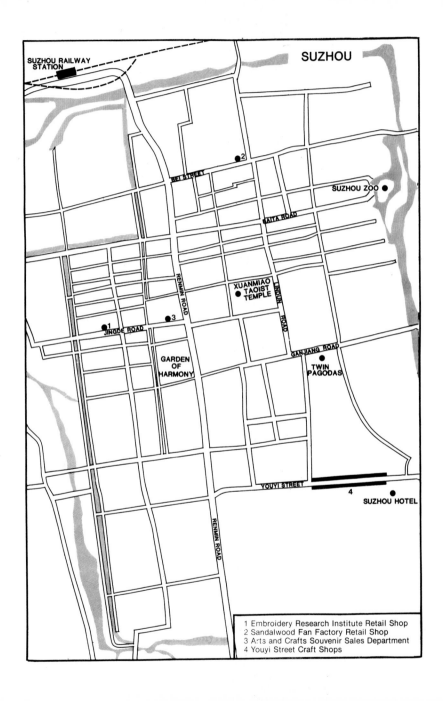

SUZHOU

SUZHOU RAILWAY STATION

BEI STREET

SUZHOU ZOO ●

BAITA ROAD

RENMIN ROAD

XUANMIAO TAOIST TEMPLE
●

LINDUN ROAD

● 2

● 3

JINGDE ROAD
● 1

GARDEN OF HARMONY

GANJIANG ROAD

TWIN PAGODAS
●

YOUYI STREET
4

SUZHOU HOTEL ●

RENMIN ROAD

1 Embroidery Research Institute Retail Shop
2 Sandalwood Fan Factory Retail Shop
3 Arts and Crafts Souvenir Sales Department
4 Youyi Street Craft Shops

Suzhou

Visitors to Suzhou will never forget the beauty of the town's white washed houses with graceful black tiled roofs whose images shine back in a luminous mosaic within the many small canals running through and around the town. Suzhou has long been praised for the lilting charm of the local speech, the beauty of its women, and its, cultured, refined style of life. As a common Chinese saying goes, "Above there is heaven and below there is Suzhou and Hangzhou."

Turn down a quiet lane and behind a plain entrance gate you will find another of Suzhou's unforgettable delights—its classical, southern–style gardens. Here retired officials and wealthy landowners once found a sumptuous retreat beside quiet pools stirred by the lazy movements of plump goldfish. Drawing inspiration from artificial hills and strangely eroded rocks as well as from pavilions overlooking carefully positioned groves of bamboo, cultured gentlemen met to share poems, drink wine, and muse on nature and man's place in it. Today the city boasts over 100 such gardens, of which about ten of the most important have been fully restored and are open to the public.

Suzhou's history stretches back 2500 years. It was the capital of the feudal state of Wu during the Spring and Autumn Period of the Zhou Dynasty. Over 1,400 years ago thousands of looms in the lower Yangzi Valley were already producing woven silk as part of a thriving industry. By the 12th century, local weavers had perfected exquisite, silk pictorial tapestries used for screen panels, hangings, and covers for scrolls and books. By the Ming Dynasty an imperial weaving workshop was established in Suzhou to create the elaborate dragon robes worn by the emperor, his close family, and court officials.

A complex symbolism of rank developed over the centuries of imperial rule, and the ceremonial robes of the emperor and his officials were one important means of its expression. The emperor was the center of the universe—indeed, he was the universe when he wore his robes, dense with cosmic symbols. The officials who stood before him at court were clearly ranked in turn by the emblems on their dragon robes. During the Ming Dynasty, these dragon robes became the embodiment of the whole Chinese feudal and imperial system. All the dragon robes incorporated symbols of prosperity, longevity, and good fortune. And all of the robes contained dragon designs embroidered on or woven in the silk.

The robes worn by the emperor were exclusive in several respects. The large, coiling, five–clawed dragons on the center front and back of the emperor's robe were his personal symbols. The emperor alone could wear all of the twelve symbols of authority, including sun, moon, stars, and earth, which date back to the most ancient Chinese ceremonial robes. Writhing dragons were woven in tapestry or embroidered with gleaming satin stitches, couched in gold thread. The dyes had to be absolutely accurate, since specific colors indicated rank and category of position. The emperor's official robes were bright yellow, although he might wear other colors. Royal princes wore red robes with dragon medallions. A single robe could easily take four or five years to complete. These were the works of master artists who made use of all their skill in design and their full appreciation of the artistic potential of silk.

During the Ming Dynasty, a number of locally–made tapestry panels were exported to Europe, where they were incorporated into the vestments used in European cathedrals. By the 19th century, Chinese figured silks were exported in endless quantity to the West, where Chinoiserie made Chinese textiles all the rage.

During the Qing Dynasty, Suzhou was designated as a special district under direct imperial control so that the production of woven and embroidered silk for the imperial household could be strictly overseen. The life of the weavers was not always fortunate, however. Silk production was highly labor–intensive and specialized, and the large majority of workers were contracted only on a daily basis. Their pay was minimal and their living conditions abysmal, which lead to numerous cases of unrest and uprisings in the 17th to 19th centuries. Nor was the lot of the average household much better. Taxes were customarily to be paid in bolts of silk, the production of which became the responsibility of the women in the household. Their difficult work has been immortalized in a poem by the great Tang Dynasty poet, Bai Juyi.

> *Liao–ling*, sheer patterned silk—what is it like?
> Not like poorer silks, *lo, shao, wan*, or *chi*,
> but the forty–five foot waterfall
> that leaps in the moonlight of Mount T'ien–t'ai;
> woven with wonderful designs:
> on a ground clothed in white mist, clustered snowflake flowers.
> Who does the weaving, who wears the robe?
> A poor woman in the glens of Yueh, a lady in the palace of Han.
> Last year eunuch envoys relayed the royal wish:
> patterns from heaven to be woven by human hands,
> woven with flights of autumn geese clearing the clouds,
> dyed with hue of spring rivers south of the Yangtze,
> cut broad for making cloak sleeves, long for sweeping skirts,
> hot irons to smooth the wrinkles, scissors to trim the seams,
> rare colors, strange designs that shine and recede again,
> patterns to be seen from every angle, patterns never in repose.
> For dancing girls of Chao–yang, token of profoundest favor,
> one set of spring robes worth a thousand in gold—
> to be stained in sweat, rouge–soiled, never worn again,
> dragged on the ground, trampled in mud—who is there to care?
> The F*liao–ling* weave takes time and toil,
> not to be compared to common *tseng* or *po*;
> thin threads endlessly plied, till the weaver's fingers ache;
> clack–clack the loom cries a thousand times but less than a foot is
>   done.
> You singers and dancers of the Chao–yang Palace,
> could you see her weaving, you'd pity her too!
> (Burton Watson, trans., in Burton Watson, *Chinese Lyricism*. New
>   York: Columbia University Press, 1971, pp.185–6)

Today Suzhou's textile workers enjoy a more comfortable, secure life, but silk production, weaving, printing, and embroidery continue to be a major industry here. Visitors may enjoy touring the city's silk weaving and silk printing mills and embroidery factory. The city is also home to one of China's two embroidery research institutes, the other being in Changsha, Hunan Province.

What to Look For

For centuries an important center of textile and silk production, Suzhou today continues to excel at single–sided, double–sided, and cross stitch embroidery as well as the modern effects achieved by new stitches. Ke–si woven silk tapestries are an intricate Suzhou specialty, along with crochet and openwork fabric decoration. Knowledgeable shoppers will look for lovely silk crepe scarves and fabric in Suzhou, printed with traditional designs and colors. The city is also known for a high level of craftsmanship in carving wood, jade, and ivory, of which a large selection is available. And for many years Suzhou has been renowned for its intricately carved folding fans of ivory and sandalwood. The colorful local clay toys, eggshell paintings, and folding lanterns also make nice souvenirs.

Where to Look

Downtown Suzhou is full of large stores and small shops carrying local and regional crafts. On Jingde Road you will find the Embroidery Research Institute and the adjacent Arts and Craft Souvenir Sales Department. If you stroll along the narrow side streets in this busy area and along Guanqian Street, you will come across many shops selling inexpensive crafts, such as toys, silk fabric, woven bamboo ware, and fans. Walking north along Lindun Road will bring you to the Sandalwood Fan Factory, which is located in a lovely old Chinese building between the Historical Museum and the North Temple Pagoda. To the south, Youyi Street runs east and west in front of the entrance to the beautiful Garden of the Master of the Fishing Nets. Between Fenghuang Street and the Suzhou Hotel Youyi Street is flanked on both sides with shops selling all manner of inexpensive Suzhou crafts. And if all this walking makes you hungry, try some of Suzhou's famous sweets. The Daoxiangcun and Caizhizhai candy stores on Guanqian Street sell all kinds of sweet cakes, candy, nuts, and preserved fruits, while the

Huangtianyuan Cake Shop at 88 Guanqian Street has been selling pastries in this location for almost 150 years.

Highly Recommended Stores ★ ★

1. **Suzhou Embroidery Research Institute Retail Shop** ★ ★
   262 Jingde Road
   Telephone: 6297

   刺绣研究所外宾服务部
   景德路262 号

   Hours: 9–6

   Accepts traveler's checks and all major credit cards

   Has English–speaking staff

   Recommended Crafts

   - double–sided embroidery of kittens or goldfish (100 *yuan* and up)
   - lustrous "paintings in silk" of traditional landscapes or birds and flowers (50 *yuan* and up)
   - framed, embroidered table screens or embroidered silk fans (25 *yuan* and up)

   For centuries Suzhou residents have been working at embroidery, creating a distinctive style of work famous for its flat surfaces, neat edges, delicacy, and closely packed stitches with even thickness and spacing. In 1957 the Suzhou Embroidery Research Institute was established to train designers and artists to research and preserve the ancient art of embroidery, while selectively modernizing some of its techniques. Craftspeople at the institute have developed thirty or so new stitches and thousands of ways of combining different colored threads. The master embroiderers here use the needle like a brush, blending long and short satin stitches to create tones and colors, slanting the stitches so that the silk floss reflects the light at different angles. In this way embroiderers can faithfully copy landscape paintings, portraits or detailed designs of any sort in embroidery.

   Double–sided embroidery, absolutely perfect on both sides, is a particular specialty of Suzhou. Using a sheet of fine, transparent silk gauze or nylon, the embroiderer works intricate pictures, all the while concealing a myriad of knots and thread ends so that the finished work is perfect on each side. The silk threads used in double–sided embroidery are split to one forty–eighth of their normal thickness, and are so fine that they are all but invisible. At the institute you can tour the studios where needleworkers, most of them young women, create exquisite silk pictures of ethereal goldfish or fluffy kittens in double–sided embroidery. Some are even able to work a different scene on each side of an embroidery.

While touring the institute you will also see brocade experts creating a traditional type of weaving called *ke–si*, or "cut silk," which had become a thriving industry in this area as early as the 12th century. The exquisite silk tapestries, which may take up to a year to complete, reproduce famous landscape or bird and flower paintings. Using a traditional wooden loom and a needle for a shuttle, the ke–si weaver separates the weft or crosswise, threads of different colors, creating spaces between the various colors which are visible when held up to the light.

The Suzhou Embroidery Research Institute also specializes in cross–stitch and newly devised stitches, such as a "tangled stitch" which is used to create depth and texture in modern–style compositions.

After viewing these fascinating techniques, visitors can purchase samples at the small retail shop on the grounds of the institute. Quality is exceptional and prices are commensurate with the high level of craftsmanship. Look for luminous paintings in embroidered silk with traditional landscapes or flowers. You may also find silk embroidery incorporated into delicate flat fans or small, framed table screens. Among the Suzhou double–sided embroideries, fluffy kittens, goldfish, and elegant women are favored subjects. Mounted in rosewood frames, the largest and most intricate double–sided embroideries may sell for tens of thousands of *yuan*. It is interesting to see that many have a small red mark on one side. This is an embroidered version of the seal of the creator.

2. Sandalwood Fan Factory Retail Shop ★ ★
58 Xibei Street
Telephone: 4982

檀香扇厂门市部
西北亍58号

Hours: 8–6 daily

Accepts traveler's checks and all major credit cards

Has English–speaking staff

Recommended Crafts

- folding fans with bamboo frames and painted landscape scenes (2–25 *yuan*)
- carved sandalwood fans (40–300 *yuan*)
- carved, seven–inch sandalwood figurines (50–200 *yuan*)

Visitors to Suzhou will enjoy a tour of the Sandalwood Fan Factory, which is housed in a striking old building that dates back to the Ming Dynasty. Flat and folding fans have been popular in China for centuries, but by the Ming folding fans took precedence as it became the custom of famous artists and calligraphers to decorate their silk or paper surfaces with painting.

Today the Suzhou fan factory employs some 200 workers. One workshop specializes in making flat fans of painted paper and silk mounted on bamboo or ivory frames. In another workshop, workers carve fine, latticework patterns on the frames of folding fans using bamboo, mahogany, sandalwood, bone, or ivory. You can even see intricate fans fashioned entirely of carved sandalwood or ivory. With each movement, the sandalwood fan conveys a cool breeze scented with the delicate aroma of sandalwood, making this material especially prized for fans.

After visiting the workshops you may wish to purchase some of the products at the retail shop, which carries almost every type of fan in silk, paper, bamboo, ivory, bone, lacquer, or sandalwood. The store also displays some extravagant items, such as carved mother–of–pearl fans, large ivory fans for wall hangings, and even ivory bird cages, which may sell for several thousand *yuan* and up. But the majority of the pieces here are quite reasonable, and it is possible to find some elaborately carved fans for as little as 2.40 to 5 *yuan*. On a recent visit I also saw small carved sandalwood figures, which are relatively rare because of the growing scarcity of sandalwood.

Recommended Stores ★

1. Suzhou Arts and Crafts Souvenir Sales Department ★
274 Jingde Road
Telephone: 2762

旅游纪念品工艺品经销部
景德路274 号

Manager: Cao Naishun

Hours: 8–6 daily

Accepts traveler's checks and all major credit cards

Has English–speaking staff

Recommended Crafts

- framed double–sided embroidery (100–5,000 *yuan*)
- traditional musical instruments
- painted eggshell scenes mounted on silk within a wooden frame
  (5–20 *yuan*) and colorful Tiger Hill clay toys (1–15 *yuan*)
- printed silk fabric and scarves (4–20 *yuan*)

If you want to find a wide selection of Suzhou's varied handicrafts under one roof, then this is the store to visit. Here are all manner of locally made silk and wool rugs, inlaid lacquer furniture and screens, traditional musical instruments, carved jade and ivory, and the "four treasures" of the artist's studio. You may also enjoy the local folk items, such as painted eggshells and brightly painted Huqiu (Tiger Hill) clay toys. The store is the largest of its kind in the city and carries many fine pieces from the Suzhou Embroidery Research Institute.

Fans are a specialty of the store. You are likely to find a full selection from the Sandalwood Fan Factory. Among textiles there are many styles of tablecloths with openwork and embroidered decoration, as well as crocheted silk blouses. Also look for inexpensive printed–silk fabrics and scarves, such as charming navy–and–cream crepe scarves with plum blossom designs for as little as 4 *yuan*. For jade lovers the store carries an extensive variety, from small rings and earrings to large sculptures for 30,000 *yuan*.

The shop is housed in a charming, traditional–style pavilion with fine carved wood details and latticed windows. Although prices may be somewhat higher here than in other outlets in Suzhou, the selection is far greater. In addition, the store is staffed by knowledgeable salespeople who are happy to assist customers with arrangements for packing and shipping.

2. Youyi Street Craft Shops ★

Located on Youyi Street between Fenghuang Street and the Suzhou Hotel

友谊路市场
友谊路在凤凰路和苏州饭店之间

Hours: stores are generally open from about 1 p.m. until 10 p.m.

Accepts cash only

Few English speakers

Recommended Crafts

- ceramic reproductions of Ming and Qing Dynasty porcelain
- embroidered silk squares and panels (15–20 *yuan*)
- medium–quality double–sided embroidery with small wooden stands (10–40 *yuan*)
- painted and carved fans (2–3 yuan)

As you walk along the section of Youyi Street between Fenghuang Street and the Suzhou Hotel you will find a haven of small shops selling local and regional crafts. The tranquil scenery of the road, shaded by plane trees as it skirts a picturesque canal, is in sharp contrast to the brisk atmosphere at the stores lining both sides of the street. Here bustling shopkeepers eagerly seek out business.

You can browse through a wide variety of items, including batik and stencil–print fabrics, silk qipao, inexpensive scrolls, fans, embroidery, and ceramic reproductions. You may have to ask to have things brought out, as displays are rather dark and cluttered. Although the quality of the merchandise may not be equal to that of the pieces in the Arts and Crafts Souvenir Sales Department, the prices can be considerably lower. In addition, bargaining is expected, which can bring the price even lower. Framed, double–sided embroideries with wooden stands are available here, although they are rougher than those at the Embroidery Institute. You may also find embroidered silk panels and squares, as well as painted and carved fans. The bustling atmosphere and free interchange make this a pleasant place to take an after–dinner stroll.

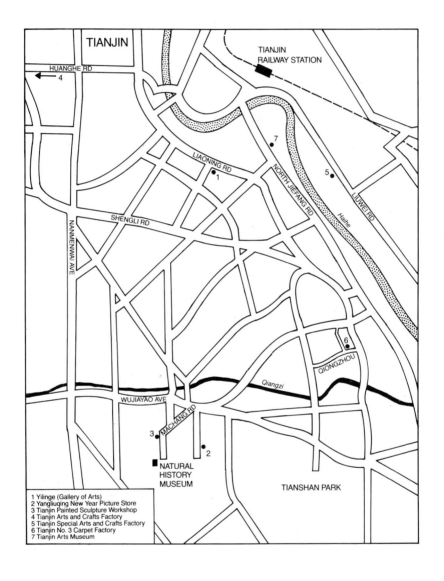

TIANJIN

HUANGHE RD

← 4

TIANJIN
RAILWAY STATION

LIAONING RD

● 1

● 7

NORTH JIEFANG RD

● 5

LIUWEI RD

Haihe

SHENGLI RD

NANMENWAI AVE

● 6

QIONGZHOU

Qiangzi

WUJIAYAO AVE

MACHANG RD

3 ●

● 2

■ NATURAL
HISTORY
MUSEUM

TIANSHAN PARK

1 Yilinge (Gallery of Arts)
2 Yangliuqing New Year Picture Store
3 Tianjin Painted Sculpture Workshop
4 Tianjin Arts and Crafts Factory
5 Tianjin Special Arts and Crafts Factory
6 Tianjin No. 3 Carpet Factory
7 Tianjin Arts Museum

Tianjin

From its earliest settlement, Tianjin has been a town connected with trade. Named Xhigu ("buy and sell") in the 12th century, Tianjin soon became a key in the transportation network connecting north China with the fertile south. Rice and tribute items were brought to Tianjin along the Grand Canal for distribution to the court at Beijing. In 1404 the city was fortified with walls and continued to grow in importance as an industrial and commercial center over the centuries that followed.

The arrival of Western powers in the 19th century saw a change in Tianjin's fortunes. In 1856 a relatively insignificant incident provoked a confrontation between China and the British, who had long been chafing against the restriction of their trade to Canton. The British sent Lord Elgin to demand an end to the Canton system of trade and the opening of new ports along the Yangzi River. Under threat of a British march on Beijing, the Chinese consented. The terms of this treaty were reinforced in 1860 by further "gunboat diplomacy" and Tianjin was opened to foreign commerce and residence.

By 1914 nine different Western concessions had been set up in Tianjin, and the city's architecture soon took on a strongly European flavor. The Astor Hotel, the Kiesling Restaurant, and the city's numerous Victorian mansions are all relics of this era.

What to Look For

A visit to Tianjin not only offers travelers a chance to purchase a number of famous traditional crafts but also provides opportunities to visit the

135

craft workshops and observe the pieces being made. Colorfully painted kites, painted clay sculptures, hand-knotted wool carpets, and vibrant New Year woodblock prints are all well-known specialties that visitors can see being made. Knowledgeable travelers will also wish to leave time for the city's antique shops, which are well stocked and not as carefully scoured as their counterparts in Beijing or Shanghai.

Although the Tianjin Art Museum is disappointing in its limited selection of crafts for sale, a stop at the museum is highly recommended in order to see older examples of the crafts sold elsewhere in the city such as antique clay sculptures by the Zhang family, kites made by the Wei family, and Yangliuqing New Year prints.

Where to Look

Tianjin's main shopping areas are found near the intersection of Heping Road and Binjiang Road at the heart of the city (in the area known as the Heping District) and along Zhongshan Road. The Yilinge Antique Store is located in the busy downtown Heping District off Heping Road. The Yangliuqing New Year Picture Society and the Painted Sculpture Studio are located near the Tianjin Guest House in the Hexi District. The Number Three Carpet Factory is located on Qiongzhou Road near Renmin (People's) Park in the Hexi District. The Arts and Crafts Factory is located at the western end of Huanghe Road in the Nankai District.

And when the whirl of shopping creates an appetite, stop at the Goubuli Baozi (Dumpling) Shop at 97 Shandong Road near the Yilinge Antique Store. Legend has it that the Goubuli ("dog doesn't care") is named for the restaurant's founder who was so poor that even a dog paid no attention to him. Today the shop is famed throughout the country for its tasty pork dumplings. Those homesick for Western food can find consolation at the Qishilin (formerly the Kiesling cafe in the old German concession) on North Jiefang Road two blocks south of the Tianjin Hotel.

Recommended Shops ★

1. Yangliuqing New Year Picture Society ★
111 Sanheli, Tonglou, Hexi District
Telephone: 702828

杨柳青画社门市部
河西区佟楼三合里111 号

Manager: Li Zhiqiang

Hours: 8–12 a.m. and 1–5 p.m. The workshop is closed Sunday, but the shop is open every day.

Accepts traveler's checks and credit cards

Has English–speaking staff

Recommended Crafts

- colorful prints of chubby children, matted with silk brocade (16 *yuan*)
- sets of 12 prints with auspicious New Year symbols or figures from Chinese legends (300–550 *yuan*)

For more than 300 years local families have thronged to the village of Yangliuqing in Tianjin's western suburbs to purchase nianhua, the brightly colored woodblock prints used to decorate homes at the lunar New Year. By tradition, New Year's is the time of renewal, both of the home and family and of the earth and its bounty. At this time all debts are to be repaid and personal affairs are to be settled so that the new year can be ushered in on a good footing.

It is the custom at the end of the year to clean the house thoroughly and replace the door gods and the decorative prints that adorn the bedrooms and kitchen. Special attention, in the past, was paid to the Lord of the Stove, who was ushered off to heaven with proper ritual and the burning of incense so that he could report on the family's behavior during the preceding year. To ensure a good report, his lips were smeared with honey so that he could say only sweet things about the family. His send off was accomplished by burning his picture so that he would be conveyed in the smoke up to heaven. In the following days fresh prints were hung to celebrate the arrival of the new year and assure its prosperity.

The most famous centers for producing these New Year prints were Weifang in Shandong Province, Taohuawu near Suzhou, and Yangliuqing. These areas continue to be important printmaking regions today. In the 17th century Yangliuqing was already famous for creating festive prints using a combination of woodblock printing and fine, realistic brushwork. The prints expressed wishes for prosperity, longevity, and good fortune in the coming year by using popular symbols such as deer (high rank and longevity), carp (success in scholarship), peonies (wealth and rank), and peaches (longevity). Other pictures used a rebus or play on words. Goldfish and lotuses, for example, conveyed the hope that one would have abundance for years in succession, through a play on words in which lian (lotus) represents lian (successive) and yu (fish) represents yu (abundance).

Visitors to the Yangliuqing New Year Picture Society may observe each stage of the painstaking pictorial process. Yangliuqing prints are unique in combining woodblock printing with hand painting. The first step is to carve blocks, which are then used to apply background color washes. Sometimes as many as forty separate blocks are required to complete the initial printing of colors. Then follows the painstaking application of additional colors and outline details, which results in paintings of striking detail and complexity.

The rooms of the society are hung floor to ceiling with colorful prints of elegant court ladies, red–cheeked, chubby children, and figures from Chinese legend and history. Kites and reproductions of famous Chinese paintings are also sold. Among the best buys are small (12") matted prints of chubby children and colorful kites. Decorative sets of twelve prints handsomely bound in silk brocade and joined with accordion pleats also make nice gifts.

Visitors are welcome to tour the workshop without special arrangements, but English–speaking guides must be requested in advance.

2. Tianjin Painted Sculpture Studio ★
202 Machang Road, Hexi District
Telephone: 334103

泥人张彩塑工作室

河西区马场道202 号

Manager: Wang Kai

Hours: 8–12 a.m. and 1–5 p.m. Closed Sunday

Accepts credit cards but not traveler's checks Staff speaks very limited English

Recommended Crafts

- large figure of peasant woman nursing her child (500 *yuan*)
- doctor of traditional Chinese medicine taking the pulse of an old man (800 *yuan*)

For more than 140 years the Zhang family's name has been synonymous with the craft of clay sculpture in Tianjin. First–generation clay sculptor Zhang Mingshan (1826–1908) established the family's reputation, which is preserved through the efforts of fourth–generation descendant Zhang Ming, who now heads the Painted Sculpture Studio.

After allied troops marched through Tianjin in the wake of the Boxer Rebellion in 1900, clay caricatures modeled with realistic facial expressions and uniform details began to appear in the marketplace. Many of these popular sculptures probably came from the hand of a descendant of Zhang Mingshan.

Today this tradition of exquisite detail and realistic modeling is preserved at the Painted Sculpture Studio. The limited scale of these sculptures, which usually do not exceed 18", challenges the sculptors to accurately depict costume, facial expression, and gestures. Some of the most popular subjects are opera characters, historical figures, and humorous people from everyday life. Visitors will delight in seeing charming scenes of the Monkey King engaged in characteristic deviltry or an elegant tableau of court beauties playing classical musical instruments. Each ornament of the headdress, each fold of the garment, is skillfully captured by the sculptor's deft fingers.

A tour of the workshops can be arranged in advance, and English–speaking interpreters secured. It is fascinating to watch the sculptors shape and paint colorful figures, but the visit to the studio may be disappointing in one respect. Only a small number of pieces on display are available for immediate purchase, and those that are available appear to be the very simplest and least inspired subjects. Prices range from 4 *yuan* to 120 *yuan*. Any of the other figures may be ordered, but the order will be referred to the original sculptor and may require as much as three months for completion.

Another drawback is that the staff is not particularly well informed, and the policy on shipping seems unclear. While one worker said that they could arrange for shipping, another said that shipping could only be handled on large orders. Be sure to check before you make a purchase.

3. Tianjin Arts and Crafts Factory ★
West end of Huanghe Road, Nankai District
Telephone: 563260

工艺美术厂
南开区黄河道

Hours: 7:30–4:30

Accepts credit cards Limited English–speaking staff

Recommended Crafts

- large kites of dragons or centipedes
- tiny miniature kites less than four inches across

Kites have been popular in China for centuries and can be traced by legend back as far as the early Warring States Period (475–221 BC). Their earliest use appears to be military, as flying machines carrying men to reconnoiter an enemy's troops. In the 9th century AD, kites were used by a minister to communicate with friendly forces outside the city. In later years kit–flying became a civilian entertainment, and small whistles were attached to the tail of the kite to produce musical tones. It is from this practice that the Chinese kite receives its name –"wind zither".

Another popular custom was to glue glass fragments to the strings and then attack another's kite. Whoever could cut the other's kite string first was declared the winner.

Today some of the finest kites are made in Shandong Province at Weifang and at Yangliuqing. The skeleton is usually made of bamboo splints to which silk or a durable paper (known as Korean paper) is attached. Great attention is paid to the designs on the kites, which are colorful and bold. Shapes include birds of all sorts, animals, human figures, dragons, insects or goldfish. Size may range from miniature kites of only several inches up to centipedes many feet long. Decorations may be either painted by hand or be produced by the woodblock printing process. When a brisk spring wind blows aloft a gray hawk with flapping wings, one can easily forget these are paper creations and not living, breathing creatures.

The Tianjin Arts and Crafts Factory today produces charming kites decorated in traditional style with colorful fish, birds, insects, or dragons. The kites are hand painted and often have bamboo whistles attached. Usually the pieces can be folded or taken apart for convenience in carrying. Prices run from about 10– to 75 *yuan*.

In addition to kites, tourists may peruse a variety of paper cuts, woodblock prints, and silk items. Tianjin is also zealous in creating shell mosaics and feather pictures of landscape scenes, but these are not to everyone's taste.

4. Yilinge (Forest of Arts) ★
161 Liaoning Road, Heping District
Telephone: 700308

艺林阁
河平区辽宁路161 号

Manager: Yu Shuying

Hours: 9–5:30 daily

Accepts traveler's checks and credit cards

Has English–speaking staff

Recommended Crafts

• antique snuff bottles –antique clocks with cloisonné decor (2,000 *yuan* and up) –silver wine flask with gold repousse design (2,200 *yuan*)

Yilinge is Tianjin's largest antique store and is famous for the broad array of its merchandise and the helpfulness of its staff. Here one can browse through antiquities dating back to the Neolithic Period. The store's graceful hardwood cabinets are crammed full of beautiful items including Shang Dynasty inscribed oracle bones, Western Zhou bronze vessels, Warring States Period bronze swords and colorful Tang sacai horses.

On the first floor one finds hardwood and inlaid furniture, new and old ceramics, and lacquerware. The second floor is a profusion of carved jade and ivory, jewelry, antique fans, and antique and contemporary scroll paintings and calligraphy. The shop is also known for its large collection of antique snuff bottles and antique clocks with cloisonné details. It is sometimes possible to find unusual antiques here of a quality unavailable in shops in Beijing or Shanghai, where the stock is more picked over.

A knowledgeable and accommodating staff makes shopping at Yilinge a pleasure. The shop will also arrange seal engravings, currency exchange, packing and insurance, as well as commissions for special pieces.

5. Tianjin No. 3 Carpet Factory ★
125 Qiongzhou Road, Hexi District
Telephone: 81712/3/4

地毯三厂

河西区琼州道125 号

Manager: Gao Guoliang

Hours: 7:30–4, closed Monday.

Accepts traveler's checks and credit cards

Has limited number of English–speaking staff

Recommended Crafts

- carpets with only two complementary colors, decorated with stylized longevity symbols or auspicious symbols such as bats, flowers, deer, phoenixes or dragons
- quietly rich monochrome carpets deeply embossed with designs of bamboo, clouds, or stylized longevity symbols

The craft of carpet–making was introduced rather late to China, probably from Central Asia and Mongolia. The earliest extant Chinese carpets date to the 8th century and are made of embroidered woolen felt. The knotting process and loom were not used in China until much later. In north and northwest China carpets of wool and silk were used as saddle blankets, wall hangings, and prayer rugs, as well as to cover the heated brick beds, or *kangs*. In 1860 a Buddhist priest set up a school in Beijing to teach the skills of knotting wool carpets. A branch of the school was subsequently established in Tianjin, which became known for durable camel wool carpets with simple designs.

Today Tianjin has a number of carpet factories where craft workers card and spin wool, knot the yarn, clip the finished carpet, and give a final chemical wash. One skilled worker may take more than a year to complete one carpet, carefully knotting colored wool yarn in the shape of a figure eight onto the warp, or vertical threads.

At the Tianjin Number 3 Carpet Factory visitors can see every stage in the process, but tours must be arranged in advance. Especially interesting are the detailed work of hand knotting and the clipping process which results in embossed effects. Established in 1905, this factory is the largest carpet factory in China. The factory produces wool carpets with 70 to 120 rows of knots ("line", in carpet parlance) per ten inches. The factory also produces a limited number of silk "art" carpets which are much more densely knotted.

Travelers in the market for a carpet should be able to find something to suit their taste and budget here. Rugs come in a variety of sizes, shapes, and prices. The average cost of a 6' x 9' carpet is 2,100 *yuan*. Smaller carpets for wall hangings cost 500 *yuan* and up.

A vast selection of patterns are available, from intricate Western aubusson floral designs to Chinese–style bird and flower pictures and ancient symbols of bronze vessels and stone rubbings. Perhaps most elegant are the pastel monochrome carpets whose only design comes from intricate embossing. A rug like this, thick and luminous, would indeed transform a room into a showplace.

It is a good idea to study patterns and prices of Chinese carpets in the United States before your China visit. The rug you select should have a minimum of 90 lines and a pile of at least 5/8". More densely knotted rugs are occasionally available, but prices will be higher per foot than the examples give above.

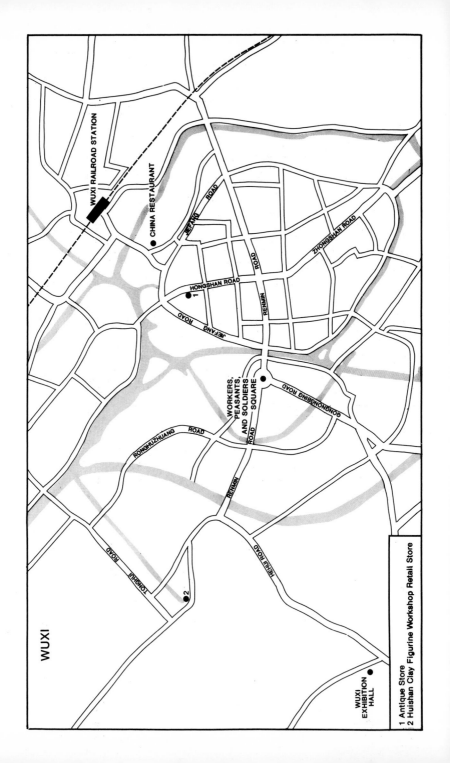

Wuxi

Located on the north shore of Lake Tai in the fertile land south of the Yangzi River, Wuxi is a picturesque city criss-crossed by canals and streams. The city dates back to the Zhou Dynasty (ca. 1066–256 BC), when tin was mined locally, giving the city its early name of Youxi, meaning "to have tin." By the Han Dynasty, when the tin supply had run out, the city assumed its current name, meaning "tinless."

In the 7th century Wuxi gained importance as a traffic hub on the newly constructed Grand Canal. Emperor Yang of the Sui Dynasty initiated the construction of this network of canals from the Yangzi River north to the region of Beijing. His objective was to ship troops, supplies and grain from the fertile south via the canal and the Yellow River to the northern capitals of Changan (present–day Xian) and Luoyang. This imaginative and vast undertaking required the labor of hundreds of thousands of workers to complete. Later historians have criticized the project as a wasteful extravagance erected only so that Emperor Yang could travel in comfort by water from his northern capitol in Luoyang to his southern palace in Yangzhou.

The system of waterways not only transported grain and supplies but carried another valuable commodity: the fantastically shaped rocks from Lake Tai which had become an essential part of the finished landscape of any Chinese garden. Punctured with eroded holes and jagged outlines, some of these rocks were more than twenty feet high. The most valuable were dredged from Lake Tai, where the constant force of the water ground small, hard stones against softer boulders to create the finest of garden rockery. It is said that the 12th century Emperor Huizong of the Song Dynasty was so obsessive in collecting such rocks for his imperial garden that the Grand Canal was blocked for days with barges carrying only this valuable cargo. Today the Grand Canal continues to play an important role in the city's transportation and economy, and its waterways bustle with all manner of vessels, from small cement punts poled by one operator to long lines of wooden, flat–bottomed barges.

Wuxi is also well known as a center for the production of silk, with all the stages of manufacture represented, from raising the silkworms to the final weaving and embroidery. In the early 20th century Shanghai industrialists brought modern technology to Wuxi, mechanizing certain stages of silk and textile production so that the city became the important textile center it is today.

What to Look For

Visitors to Wuxi will find an attractive array of woven silk products for sale, as well as beautifully embroidered silk and linen items. For over 1,500 years the Wuxi area has specialized in silk production, and today the city boasts several silk–reeling mills. From spring to fall it is possible to visit a local commune to see the time–consuming traditional process of raising silkworms, which requires feeding the voracious creatures a constant supply of fresh mulberry leaves until they begin to spin their cocoons. At a silk–reeling mill, you can see the laborious process of making finished silk. First the cocoons are separated by grade and then soaked in boiling water to dissolve the sticky sericin which surrounds the thread. The long, fine, continuous fiber is then twisted and reeled onto spools. These are generally tended by young women who run back and forth to release tangled threads. When one considers that an ounce of silkworm eggs produces 30,000 silkworms, which then consume a ton of mulberry leaves to yield twelve pounds of raw silk, one can only be surprised that silk is as inexpensive as it is in China.

Another famous Wuxi craft is the sculpting of Huishan clay figures, made from a fine local clay which is easily modelled and dries to a very hard finish. These brightly painted sets of opera characters or gods of good fortune and longevity are popular throughout China. Knowledgeable visitors will also look for the charming unglazed "purple sand" teapots made at nearby Yixing and often available in Wuxi. Another local specialty, hand carved pipes, is available in any hotel shop, craft or department store.

Where to Look

In the bustling downtown area of Wuxi, the visitor will find a variety of stores selling local and regional crafts. The Wuxi Antique Store is located just south of Dongfanghong (East is Red) Square in the main shopping district, where one will also find the Dongfanghong Department Store and an arts and crafts store. The Friendship Store is just a short walk from here. The Huishan Clay Figurine Workshop is located in the western part of Wuxi, near Xihui Park.

Recommended Stores ★ Stores

1. Wuxi Antique Store ★
466 Zhongshan Road
Telephone: 26520

无锡古玩店
中山路466号

Hours: 7:30–11:30 a.m. and 2–5:30 p.m. daily; in winter, afternoon hours are 1–5 p.m.

Accepts traveler's checks and all major credit cards

Has English–speaking staff

Recommended Crafts

- carved stone pendants (9 *yuan*) and necklaces (15–25 *yuan*)
- reproductions of Tang polychrome glazed ceramic horses (3.5 *yuan*)

Located in a beautiful two–story building with traditional style architecture and decoration, this branch of the Wuxi Antique Store specializes in reasonably priced reproductions of famous crafts. You can find a very good selection of ceramic pieces here as well as carvings in wood, semi–precious stone, and ivory. On a recent trip we saw carved stone pendants of fairly good workmanship for 9 *yuan* and necklaces of green stone for 15 to 25 *yuan*. Reproductions of Tang Dynasty polychrome glazed horses made in Luoyang were available for as little as 3.5 *yuan*, while crackle–glazed celadon vases were 35 *yuan*. You will want to avoid some of the modern ceramic souvenir items of fat babies and contemporary figures, however, which are unimaginative and rather unattractive.

2. Huishan Clay Figurine Workshop ★
Hui Hill, Baoshanqiao

Telephone: 26669

惠山泥人厂门市部
惠山宝善桥

Hours: 7:30–4:30 daily

Accepts cash only

Has English–speaking staff

Recommended Crafts

- intoxicated Daoist immortals (a set of 8 for 12.30 *yuan*)
- the God of Longevity carrying the peaches of immortality (2 *yuan*)
- miniature set of traditional Chinese musical instruments (a set of 6 for 5.25 *yuan*)

In Wuxi the craft of making small, brightly painted clay figures began over 400 years ago during the Ming Dynasty. Local peasants were the first to discover the excellent properties of the clay found at nearby Hui Hill in the western part of Wuxi, and they used this medium to produce lively folk toys for sale at regional markets and temple fairs. As with many other types of folk art, professional craftsmen later became involved and developed a more polished, regularized type of ware based upon the folk roots. In Wuxi, too, the sculpting of clay folk toys soon became an art of professional craftsmen who chose their subjects from the popular regional opera. After 1949, this craft was taken up for study in arts and crafts research institutes, and more than 200 types of figurines have since been developed. Some pieces retain their folk character, while others are very sophisticated sculptures in the tradition of porcelain figures.

Today travelers can visit the workshop and see the sculpture and painting process. There is also a small retail outlet selling products of the workshop, which now include sculptures in dough and plaster as well as clay. On a recent visit I saw some lively little figures of intoxicated Daoist immortals, the God of Longevity carrying the peaches of immortality, and a miniature set of traditional Chinese musical instruments. With their bright colors and careful painted details, Huishan figurines make attractive souvenirs of Wuxi.

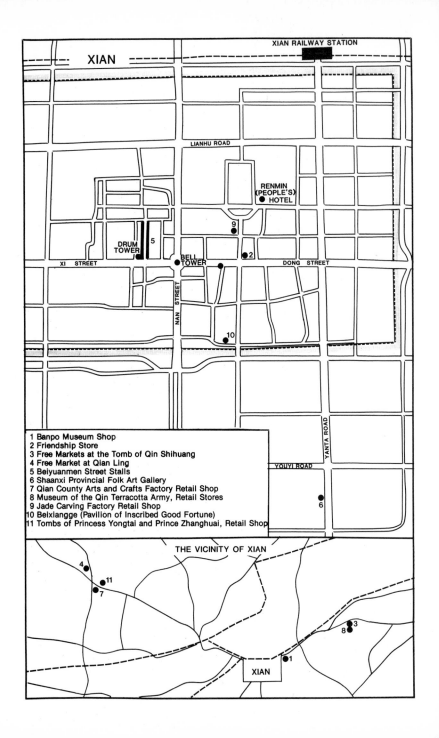

XIAN

XIAN RAILWAY STATION

LIANHU ROAD

RENMIN
(PEOPLE'S)
● HOTEL

9

DRUM
TOWER   5

BELL
TOWER

XI   STREET

2

DONG   STREET

NAN   STREET

10

YANTA ROAD

YOUYI ROAD

6

1 Banpo Museum Shop
2 Friendship Store
3 Free Markets at the Tomb of Qin Shihuang
4 Free Market at Qian Ling
5 Beiyuanmen Street Stalls
6 Shaanxi Provincial Folk Art Gallery
7 Qian County Arts and Crafts Factory Retail Shop
8 Museum of the Qin Terracotta Army, Retail Stores
9 Jade Carving Factory Retail Shop
10 Beixiangge (Pavilion of Inscribed Good Fortune)
11 Tombs of Princess Yongtai and Prince Zhanghuai, Retail Shop

THE VICINITY OF XIAN

4

11

7

8 3

1

XIAN

Xian

Through the steep, layered hills of Shaanxi Province in the central part of northern China, the Yellow River threads its way among desert wastes and mountains of yellow earth raked by erosion into fantastic sculptures and deep ravines, through high plateaus of fertile, wind–blown loess soil to the basin of the Wei River. The Wei River valley is China's cultural birthplace, where amid the natural protection of mountains and plateaus to south, west, and north the country's earliest civilization flowered. It was here that neolithic villagers wove their first cloth and decorated their pottery with delicate paintings of fish and animals, swirling clouds, and abstract patterns.

Nestled in a fertile basin of the Wei River valley, the city of Xian has witnessed a vast parade of Chinese dynasties, the rise and fall of imperial fortunes, and recurrent trespasses of nomadic tribes from the west. Today the traveler sees evidence of this past everywhere. Sections of the massive Ming Dynasty city walls of weathered gray brick still stand sentinel over the city, and man–made hills, large and small, rise above the neighboring plains, concealing the remains of ancient kings and a wealth of bronze and jade still to be unearthed. In the northwestern corner of the city, Ozymandian vestiges of the pounded earth city walls of Han emperors rise amid green wheat fields. You can feel the very pull of the past like a tangible force in this city, which dates back over 3,000 years and has stood as capital, albeit intermittently, under eleven dynasties.

Perhaps most exciting for visitors is the army of life–size clay archers, foot soldiers, cavalry, and horses which watches over the tomb of China's first unifier, Qin Shihuang. This was the mighty emperor who laid the foundations for a unified China, who standardized the Chinese written language, and who oversaw the joining of the various walls of the feudal states to form one Great Wall. According to an account by the noted historian Sima Qian, written about a century after the emperor's death, a labor force of more than 700,000 convicts was marshalled to build the Qin emperor's palaces and to work on his tomb at Mount Li (Li Shan).

As soon as the First Emperor became king of Chin, excavations and building had been started at Mount Li, while after he won the empire more than seven hundred thousand conscripts from all parts of the country worked there. They dug through three subterranean streams and poured molten copper for the outer coffin, and the tomb was filled with models of palaces, pavilions and offices, as well as fine vessels, precious stones and rarities. Artisans were ordered to fix up crossbows so that a thief breaking in would be shot. All the country's streams, the Yellow River and the Yangtse were reproduced into a miniature ocean. The heavenly constellations were shown above and the regions of the earth below. The candles were made of whale oil to ensure their burning for the longest possible time.

The Second Emperor decreed, "It is not right to send away those of my father's ladies who had no sons." Accordingly all these were ordered to follow the First Emperor to the grave. After the interment someone pointed out that the artisans who had made the mechanical contrivances might disclose all the treasure that was in the tomb; therefore after the burial and sealing up of the treasures, the middle gate was shut and the outer gate closed to imprison all the artisans and labourers, so that no one came out. Trees and grass were planted over the mausoleum to make it seem like a hill.(Yang Hsien–yi and Gladys Yang, trans., *Selections from Records of the Historian*, by Sima Qian, Beijing: Foreign Languages Press, 1979, p.186.)

Later historical accounts recorded that the tomb was subsequently robbed and destroyed soon after the overthrow of the dynasty, a belief which was widely held until recently. Archeological investigations in 1985, however, have indicated that the layer of clay enclosing the tomb is intact, as are the walls of this "underground palace."Archeologists also have discovered a high concentration of mercury in the soil of the tomb and surrounding area, suggesting that Sima Qian's description of rivers of mercury in the tomb was accurate. As one walks in the grove of persimmon trees covering the tumulus, by paths where local peasants sell crafts to visiting tourists, one can only wonder what extraordinary treasures lie beneath one's feet. When the tomb is finally opened, China's art history will no doubt have to be rewritten once again.

Xian continued to be a strategic center in later dynasties. During the first part of the Han Dynasty, from 206 BC to 8 AD, the imperial capital was maintained at Xian, which was then called Changan, or "Eternal Peace." The splendors of the city during this prosperous era have been sung by generations of Chinese poets. In an age of stability and expansion, Han emperors sent official expeditions to Central Asia, and through these ventures, contact was eventually made with Rome and the Middle East. A thriving trade in silk was thus established.

Xian once again returned to prominence during the Tang Dynasty, in the 7th century, when the capital was re–established here and redesignated "Changan." With the founding of this dynasty, China's borders were once again secured, trade with Central Asia flourished, and Changan again became the cosmopolitan center for commerce and culture. The reign of the Tang Emperor Xuanzong saw a brilliant flowering of poetry, literature, and painting which marked the high point of the dynasty and, many would argue, of China's history as a whole. But producing the luxuries required by the court took a heavy toll on the country's resources. It is said, for example, that over 700 weavers were kept working full time just to provide silk gowns for Xuanzong's pampered favorite, the concubine Yang Guifei. As he grew totally infatuated with his concubine, the emperor paid less and less attention to pressing affairs of state. In 755 An Lushan, a frontier general of non–Chinese origins, lead a revolt and moved swiftly to attack Changan. The emperor and his concubine fled, but outside the city his imperial troops refused to follow until Yang Guifei was murdered. One of the most stirring Chinese poems ever written, Bai Juyi's "Song of Everlasting Sorrow," records this sad episode.

> …High rose Li Palace, entering blue clouds,
> And far and wide the breezes carried magical notes
> Of soft song and slow dance, of string and bamboo music.
> The Emperor's eyes could never gaze on her [Yang Guifei]
>   enough—

Till war–drums, booming from Yu–yang, shocked the whole earth
And broke the tunes of "The Rainbow Skirt and the Feathered
    Coat."
The Forbidden City, the nine–tiered palace, loomed in the dust
From thousands of horses and chariots headed southwest.
The imperial flag opened the way, now moving and now pausing—
But thirty miles from the capital, beyond the western gate,
The men of the army stopped, not one of them would stir
Till under their horses' hoofs they might trample those
    moth–eyebrows...
Flowery hairpins fell to the ground, no one picked them up,
And a green and white jade hair–tassel and a yellow–gold
    hair–bird.
The Emperor could not save her, he could only cover his face.
And later when he turned to look, the place of blood and tears
Was hidden in a yellow dust blown by a cold wind.
(Translated by Witter Bynner in Cyril Birch, ed., *Anthology of
    Chinese Literature*, New York: Grove Press, 1967, p. 267.)

With the fall of the Tang Dynasty in 907, Xian's strategic importance waned and its brilliance was eclipsed as China's focus of power
shifted permanently to the South and East. But the memories of past
greatness have been echoed by poet and painter down to the present.

What to Look For

Because of Xian's long period of dominance in Chinese history, many
significant archeological discoveries have been made here. The remarkable artifacts which have been unearthed from tombs in the area have
today become the basis for a flourishing industry in archeological reproductions. Visitors to Xian will find a wide variety of high quality craft
reproductions, such as painted neolithic pottery, life–size Qin terra cotta
figures, polychrome glazed Tang funeral wares, and lively Tang tomb
murals.

Although some of these crafts may be found elsewhere in China,
others—such as reproductions of painted neolithic pottery and Tang
tomb murals—are less commonly available. Local free markets often
sell such reproductions inexpensively, although some of these pieces

may be factory seconds. When in Xian, knowledgeable travelers will look for reproductions of the robust local celadons known as Yaozhou celadons, decorated with incised patterns of peonies, lotuses, or dragons and thickly covered with glazes in a range of green and olive tones. The city is also a good source for stone rubbings.

In addition to its historical reproductions, Xian is known for its rich diversity of folk crafts. Through centuries of change, of political turmoil and economic vigor followed by inexorable decline, the local people have maintained their traditional skills in needlework, ceramic production, papercutting, and print making. Today you can find an exciting range of folk art sold in the city's shops and free markets.

Children's clothing is especially attractive here, appliquéd or embroidered with colorful symbols such as tigers, fish, lotuses, pomegranates, and other auspicious designs. Embroidered tiger hats, slippers, pillows, and toys reveal the creativity and imaginative individuality of their makers. Other folk crafts to look for are appliquéd children's vests, soft sculptures of gourds, flowers, and animals used as charms for babies, as well as old opera skirts and "cloud collars" with embroidered panels. You may also come across small silver figures of the eight Daoist immortals designed to be sewn on a baby's hat, or a bride's wedding slippers with colorful, appliquéd designs sewn onto the bottom of the sole.

With its relatively large Hui, or Moslem, population, Xian is also a good source for Moslem embroidered caps and appliquéd vests and skirts for women. Look for the charming ceramic folk toys and whistles made in nearby Fengxiang County and distinctive daily–use ceramic jars and dishes decorated with fluid, floral patterns in blue strokes against a white background. Carved and painted leather figures used in the local shadow theater are another specialty not commonly available in other parts of China.

Where to Look

Outside of the privately run stalls on Beiyuanmen Street, there is no one area in Xian where craft shops are clustered. Some key stores are located at the sites of important archeological excavations, such as Banpo Neolithic Village, the site of the Qin terra cotta army, and the tombs of

Princess Yongtai and Prince Zhanghuai. Xian is unusual in having a special outlet for the sale of authentic folk arts, and visitors will also find that the Friendship Store carries a good selection of distinctive local crafts and archeological reproductions.

Some of the most exciting transactions, however, take place at Xian's free markets. Free wheeling, noisy, and crowded, these free markets are located near most of the important cultural and archeological sites such as the Qin terra cotta army exhibition hall and the unexcavated tomb of the Qin emperor, as well as the mausoleum of the Tang Emperor Gaozong and his empress Wu Zetian. You can spend a fascinating several hours at the privately run stalls on Beiyuanmen Street in Xian's Moslem district, where vendors do a brisk business in all kinds of fabric toys, vests, shoes, hats, and bags, along with souvenirs and special Moslem foods. Hours at these markets are variable depending on the weather and other work responsibilities.

Bargaining is the order of the day at the free markets, and prices may go down as much as 40% by the time a deal is struck. Although vendors are quite eager to solicit your attention, they seldom become overly aggressive. Equally the case, if you feel a price is too high, it is probably better to bow out gracefully rather than decry the price as unreasonable. It is also worth keeping in mind that few vendors speak English, and those who do, speak only a little. Try to limit yourself to basic, simple phrases with a liberal use of hand gestures to indicate price.

When you have agreed on the final price, indicate this clearly with the correct number of fingers, so that there is no misunderstanding after the money has changed hands. You may be uncomfortable with the whole process, in which case you can do your shopping at regular stores with fixed prices. You are not alone in this attitude, as many educated Chinese find the bargaining at these free markets to be backward and the whole idea to be somewhat embarrassing. You may even find that your Chinese guide will not want to take you there.

Highly Recommended Stores ★ ★

1. Banpo Museum Retail Shops ★ ★
Banpo Neolithic Site
Telephone: 39460

半坡博物馆外宾服务部
半坡村

Hours: 8–6 daily

Accepts traveler's checks and major credit cards

Has English–speaking staff

Recommended Crafts

- reproductions of neolithic Banpo painted pottery, such as bowls and pots (6–10 *yuan*)
- colorfully painted clay animals from Fengxiang and Qian counties (10–25 *yuan*)
- sets of clay whistles (under 5 *yuan*)

6,000 years ago a moated Chinese village was located six miles east of present–day Xian on the bank of the Chan River. Its Stone–Age inhabitants cultivated millet and planted vegetables and hemp using carved stone adzes and shovels. They fished in nearby rivers using fish hooks and spears carved from animal bones. They steamed food in earthenware tripod cooking vessels. For clothing, they wore woven hemp garments sewn with carved bone needles. The women adorned themselves with earrings, beads, hairpins and rings made of shell and bone. Using vertical and horizontal kilns they fired earthenware jars, bowls, and water basins of red clay painted with black designs depicting wild deer, long–tailed birds, fish, frogs, and insects. And when they died, they were buried in graves with the utensils and ornaments which they had used while alive.

Today one can get a fascinating glimpse of this ancient community at the Banpo Neolithic Site outside Xian. The site contains 45 home foundations, 6 pottery kilns, 200 storage pits and 250 graves, and presents an extraordinarily comprehensive picture of ancient village life in north China. Walking through the exhibition rooms at the entrance to the site, one finds dioramas and explanations of village life, how homes were constructed, how the villagers fashioned tools, utensils, and ornaments, and how they worked their pottery kilns. The explanations in these halls are especially useful because they have been translated into excellent, accurate English. From this exhibition area one moves into the covered excavation itself. Here are the original dirt foundations of houses and storage pits, as well as a modern reconstruction of what one of the homes would have looked like. Moving along a raised walkway around the site, one feels the sense of Xian's ancient past, of its inventive early ancestors who had developed stone spinning wheels, bone needles, weaving shuttles, beautifully painted coil pottery, and even a basic system of writing using over 100 simple strokes.

We highly recommend that before leaving Banpo, visitors stop at the two unprepossessing shops at the bottom of the stairs near the entrance. Here you can find a selection of some of the unusual ceramics and folk art of the region, from reproductions of neolithic jars and pots to rustic, clay folk toys and whistles. The shops sell distinctive reproductions of the red clay neolithic pots discovered in the excavation, but unfortunately they often seem to be in short supply. The original pieces were made by kneading clay into long coils and then looping it spirally around a stone or a pottery mold to form the desired shape. It is interesting that the shapes of early woven textiles can still be seen on some of these vessels, giving information about the weaving skills of these ancient people.

The ceramic decorations include impressed or incised patterns as well as small clay sculptures of human and animal heads on the lids of some vessels. Most distinctive, however, are the painted black designs of fish and animals, and the abstract swirls and geometric patterns adorning others. In an odd way some of these abstract bowls look startlingly modern. One of the best known Banpo discoveries is a bowl decorated with a human head surrounded by fish designs. Chinese scholars suggest that this represents a man, probably some sort of magician or shaman, wearing a fish–shaped headdress and engaged in rites to ensure that the village would have an abundance of fish.

Another type of ceramic to look for at the Banpo shops is a variety of colorfully painted clay animals made in nearby Qian and Fengxiang counties. These figures are hand formed without using molds and then painted with fanciful designs. Particularly popular are the tiger figures, which tradition holds are able to repel evil spirits and bring good fortune to a household. Wall plaques of tiger faces are often hung in the main room of a peasant household. Their fierce miens are softened by bird and butterfly designs attached at the ears and cheeks and by pomegranates, lotuses and peonies painted with freehand strokes on forehead, ears, and chin. These same flowers, emblematic of fertility, purity, and success in livelihood, also adorn the colorful seated tigers which are given by local grandparents as gifts to their one–month–old grandchildren.

The residents of Liuying village in Fengxiang County are well known for their skill in making such robust clay figures. Almost every household in the village has at least one member specializing in this folk art, and most of the artists are women. In addition to tigers, their favorite subjects include opera characters, resting oxen, the eight Daoist immortals, fat children riding oxen and deer, and the three gods of good fortune, wealth, and longevity. These three gods are sculpted as one body, connected side by side because they are considered to be three inseparable elements which together bring happiness. The local villagers present these figurines to relatives and friends on holidays, birthdays, and weddings as a token of good wishes. You may also find painted, black clay whistles from Xian County, which is known for making two–inch miniatures of dogs and opera characters that make noise when blown through a hole in the top of each figure. This local tradition of making clay whistles goes back as far as neolithic times, as seen in the clay whistles excavated at Banpo village. If you are lucky, you may also be able to find colorful and robust wood–block prints made at Fengxiang to hang at the entrance to the house during the lunar New Year.

2. Xian Friendship Store ★ ★
Nanxin Street
Telephone: 23749

友谊商店
南新丁

Manager: Li Yongcai

Hours: 10 a.m.–9:00 p.m. daily

Accepts traveler's checks and all major credit cards

Has English–speaking staff

Recommended Crafts

- reproductions of figures from the Qin Emperor's terra cotta funerary army (25–300 *yuan*)
- polychrome glazed Tang Dynasty tomb ceramics of animal and human figures (30 *yuan* and up)
- silk paintings of Tang tomb murals
- rubbings, especially those of the Tang imperial battle chargers
- undyed cotton peasant jackets

Like other Friendship Stores in China, the Xian branch carries a wide selection of jade and other stone carvings, cloisonné, embroidery and paintings. What makes this store unusual, however, is that in addition to these fairly standard craft items, the Xian Friendship Store stocks a variety of distinctive local crafts, folk art, and reproductions of the striking archeological relics found in and near the city. It is also worth noting that some of these items can be purchased here more cheaply than at other outlets.

If you have time to go to only one store in the city (which is often the case given the hurried schedules of many tour groups) and you want to see a little bit of everything, then this is the best store to visit. There are over 8,000 items sold here, including more than 1,000 different reproductions of the archeological finds of this region. For example, the store carries 20 different replicas of the figures from the Qin Emperor's terra cotta funerary army, ranging from several inches to lifesize.

Another local craft specialty sold in this store is the reproductions of Tang Dynasty tomb frescoes from the 17 satellite tombs near Qian Ling, the Mausoleum of Emperor Gaozong and Empress Wu Zetian. With a realistic outline style, these murals present a vivid picture of aristocratic life during the Tang Dynasty. Hunting parties, polo matches, dances, and official processions are all set down with fine strokes enlivened in a palette of earth colors. These murals, reproduced on silk, capture the feeling of the Tang originals and make wonderful yet inexpensive gifts. The store also carries northern style papercuts with their characteristic vigor and bold outlines, often incorporating humorous designs.

With the excavation of the numerous Tang tombs in the area, there has emerged a dazzling array of terra cotta funerary objects with characteristic dripped polychrome glazes. Whether depicting foreign merchants, camels and grooms, fashionably plump court ladies or pacing horses, each piece seems to breathe with its own life. The Xian Friendship Store carries over 50 different types of these polychrome figures made at the Qian County Arts and Crafts Factory.

Rubbings are another Xian specialty which visitors can find at the Friendship Store. These inexpensive prints made from the impressions of stone carvings come in a variety of subjects, from solemn banquet scenes to warriors mounted on horses that seem to fly into battle. Such rubbings derive their beauty from the skills of the stone carver. To make the rubbing, an engraved stone base is covered with moistened paper which is then gently tapped into the carved depressions with a stiff brush or leather–covered mallet. After the paper has dried, Chinese ink is applied with a special tamper. Then the finished rubbing is peeled away from the stone. The images which result may be of two types: relief designs and incised images. In the case of relief designs, the background has been carved away, leaving raised lines which emerge as black or colored patterns. With an incised image, the rubbing will show engraved areas in white and the background surface in color or black.

In many cases, the rubbing presents a clearer expression of the carved image than does the original sculpture. In addition, rubbings can capture subtle gradations of texture and the weathering of the stone surface. This graphic appearance of texture conveys the mass and age of the stone medium in a way which a simple painted reproduction could not, and this quality has become part of the unique beauty and appeal of Chinese rubbings.

Charming rubbings come from Han Dynasty sculptures in this area. Dynamic scenes carved in stone were an important decoration on the stone slabs of underground burial chambers and on stone offering shrines showing vivid scenes of daily life and the spirit realm. Architectural tiles at the end of the roof eaves were also decorated during the Han Dynasty with swirling figures of animals and legendary heroes. Xian specializes in rubbings made from these ceramic roof decorations.

Some of the most striking Chinese rubbings have come from bas–reliefs at the mausoleum of the 7th century emperor Taizong, founder of the Tang Dynasty. These large reliefs, said to be made from paintings by the famous Tang artist Yan Liben, depict the emperor's six beloved battle chargers. The powerful creatures embody the spirit of strength and loyalty to their master, moving with forceful dignity even under attack and carrying numerous arrows protruding from their flanks. It is a reflection of China's bitter past that two of the finest reliefs are no longer in China, but are now housed at the University Museum in Philadelphia. And two of the reliefs remaining in China are scarred by huge cracks made to cut the blocks into smaller pieces in order to take them out of China. Viewing the original reliefs and the two copies at the Shaanxi Provincial Museum in Xian is a history lesson in itself.

The Friendship Store carries over 300 types of rubbings, including rubbings of the Tang chargers. These large prints, 5' by 6', record the horses' fierce strength and undying loyalty. Tang people had an especially deep love for horses and these pieces are a most magnificent expression of that love.

Before you leave the store, take a look at the cotton T–shirts and undyed peasant work jackets on the first floor. Shaanxi is famous for the production of cotton. Its cotton knits are particularly fine and soft, although they will shrink a great deal with their first washing. The attractive, simple, ecru peasant jackets with traditional closings are the same as those worn with bold waist sashes by farmers at work in the fields. At 5.10 *yuan* they are a great buy, extremely comfortable, and generously cut so they will fit almost anyone. They are also enthusiastically received as gifts.

3. Xian's Free Markets ★ ★

In recent years free markets where private vendors sell their wares or food items have surged back into importance in China. In Xian there are a number of these markets, which are usually located near important cultural or acheological sites visited by foreign tourists. These are places to browse and mingle, touch and compare, scrutinize and haggle. There is almost always an air of crowding, bustling, energetic, and noisy humanity at these free markets. It is a warm, enjoyable experience which the Chinese call *renao*—"hot and noisy."

Most of the folk crafts sold at Xian's free markets are textiles. Whether hat, shoes, bibs, vest, or toys, the tiger is the predominant design on these objects. In Chinese folk tradition the tiger is credited with the ability to drive off or devour evil spirits and to protect the wearer from harm and sickness. These tiger garments were also thought to confer the strength and bravery of the tiger on the wearer, so that such items were usually meant to be worn by little boys. The tiger designs are never frightening, however. Their ears are pricked up alertly to represent their intensity, and their eyes are large and staring. Superstition held that the eyes should be shiny to deflect evil influences from the child. On the tiger's forehead is usually placed the Chinese character for king, *wang*, 王, to show its status as king among animals.

There are several traditional holidays when such gifts are given. New babies are presented with an array of gifts in celebration of reaching their first full month. As part of the "full month" celebration, it used to be the custom for the child's family to prepare a feast and entertainment for relatives and friends, who in turn presented clothes and toys with auspicious figures, especially of tigers. Stuffed cotton tiger pillows, hats with tiger faces, tiger slippers and tiger bibs are still presented on this occasion in many rural areas of China. Another traditional gift for this celebration was silver jewelry in the stylized shape of a lock. Beautifully decorated with bats, butterflies, and other auspicious symbols, these locks were hung from red silk cord or mounted on a silver necklace and worn to "lock the child to life" and preserve him from harm. Any family with sufficient means would provide these for a son, but much less frequently for a daughter, reflecting the low status of women in old Chinese society. Another "full month" gift was small, flat plates of silver hammered into figures of the God of Longevity or the eight Daoist immortals. Tiny holes around the edges of the figures permitted them to be sewn to a baby's cap. Although these charming figures are seldom made today in China, you may come across some old ones at Xian's free markets or antique stores.

Silk charms filled with fragrant herbs and hung with long tassels are another folk craft which you are sure to see at the free markets here. These charms were traditionally made to celebrate the Dragon Boat Festival on the fifth day of the fifth lunar month. During this hot season, insects proliferated and were thought to carry disease. In particular, there were "five poisonous creatures" to be feared: scorpion, centipede, lizard, toad, and snake. The "fragrant pouches," as they are called in Chinese, were thought to repel the five poisonous creatures that might threaten a child. The charms were often made into the shape of a gourd, which was associated with fertility, abundance, longevity and mystical Daoist powers. It is fascinating that earthenware vases in the shape of double gourds were excavated at the nearby Banpo Neolithic village, documenting the ancient origins of the gourd as a form of craft decoration.

Other silk charms are hung from appliquéd soft sculptures of little boys sitting on lotuses carrying a reed pipe and cassia flowers. By a play on words, these objects symbolize the hope that a family might have a succession of sons attaining high official position. Fish are also popular symbols, again because of a play on words in which the word for fish, yu, sounds like the word for abundance, *yu* (written with a different Chinese character). Other crafts connected with the Dragon Boat Festival are colorfully embroidered bibs or appliquéd vests with the five poisonous creatures worked against a red background. By the process of appliquéing or embroidering these dreaded figures on a vest, it was believed that their power to harm was overcome.

Among the various free markets, I will list some of my favorites. It bears repeating that this is just a general indication of the markets, because their location and times are quite variable depending on weather, farming activities, and government directives. As you would expect, sales here are by cash only; no traveler's checks or credit cards are accepted.

Free Markets at the Tomb of Qin Shihuang

The archeological excavations of the Qin emperor's terra cotta army have become one of the must–see stops for tourists to China. Thousands visit the site every month, which makes this a logical place for a free market selling crafts for foreigners. If you are looking for reproductions of the Qin figures, we suggest that you first visit the museum stores to get an idea of the variety and prices of the items sold there. Then you you can compare these with what is available from the private vendors nearby. There are two market areas here. One is directly outside the gates to the excavation complex. The other is farther away in the second parking lot. Both are easy to spot and are open roughly the same hours as the exhibition itself, weather permitting.

Rows upon rows of stalls display all shapes and sizes of terra cotta reproductions, from 3" figures for 0.90 *yuan* to 18" figures for 10 *yuan*. These are considerably cheaper than the reproductions sold at the museum stores inside the exhibition area, but some of these free market pieces are seconds. However, if you choose carefully and examine everything thoroughly before purchasing, you will be quite satisfied with the objects from the free market.

In addition to reproductions of the Qin figures, you can find other local folk arts here. Appliquéd and embroidered children's vests are 6 to 7 *yuan*, children's tiger shoes are 4 *yuan*, and toys are 1 to 2 *yuan*. Also look for tiger hats and bibs. If you show any interest, vendors will pull out old pieces which are "family heirlooms," some of which can be quite interesting. Old glasses with round silver frames, snuff boxes, cosmetic chests, and opera costume collars can be found this way, as well as silver or pewter opium pipes (60 *yuan*) or old, embroidered silk dresses (30–40 *yuan*). Vendors will compete for your business here, and bargaining is expected.

There are also peasants who sell similar crafts at the Qin emperor's mausoleum, which has yet to be excavated, about one mile west of where the terra cotta figures were found.

Free Market at Qian Ling

Located about 50 miles west of Xian, Qian Ling is the site of the mausoleum of Emperor Gaozong and Empress Wu Zetian. When tour buses arrive here, peasants and children who live nearby often bring out crafts for sale. The range is similar to that seen in the free markets of the city, but you may find more old pieces. The colorfully embroidered panels which decorate the collars of opera costumes are a popular item, as well as long opera skirts.

Stalls on Beiyuanmen Street

Probably the largest area of private enterprise is found on Beiyuanmen Street near the Drum Tower, in Xian's Moslem section. This street is only one of ten residential streets which the city has planned to convert to private businesses connected with the tourist trade. Over 100 of the 176 families living on Beiyuanmen Street have already opened shops selling souvenirs and handmade crafts.

The atmosphere here is unique. Small stalls fronting both sides of the street stock all kinds of colorful toys, textiles and souvenirs. In addition to shoes, bags, pillows, and jackets, look for old tiger hats embroidered with gold threadand decorated with long flaps down the back (4–8 *yuan*). You can also find colorfully appliquéd vests with dragons and the five poisonous creatures, charming oilpaper umbrellas, and Fengxiang painted ceramic animals. You may come across very inexpensive reproductions of Tang dripped glaze ceramics. Check them carefully before you buy, as they may be factory seconds. As long as their defects are not visible, you will have found quite a bargain.

If you ask, some of the vendors will bring out old Qing opera costume pieces to sell. Also look for roughly–incised silver figures of the Eight Immortals used on babies' hats. Another interesting craft here is the beautifully embroidered style of cap worn by Moslems in Xian. While you are shopping, you might also like to sample some of the Islamic food sold along the street.

The Beiyuanmen stalls are open daily from about 7 a.m. to 10 p.m.You might try simple English here, as many of the vendors are working to learn English to use in negotiating with their foreign clientele. Although a good deal of the merchandise is souvenir items—T–shirts, postcards, bags—visiting the Beiyuanmen market is still a fascinating experience.

Recommended Crafts

In looking at the crafts described above, you will see that quality can vary considerably, depending on the skill of the individual maker. Check textiles for care in needlework and evenness of stitches. Look for spotting, fraying, or holes in the fabric. With baby shoes, for example, look at the hand sewn soles; in the best shoes, the soles are hand quilted in a regular diamond pattern which is quite lovely. You will also probably want to steer away from folk crafts which incorporate a great deal of machine work or non–handmade decoration, such as machine made ribbon, ric–rac, or plastic buttons for eyes. Also look at the design of the objects. There is great latitude for individual expression and creativity in folk art. Do the tiger faces capture the vigor and life of their subject or do they look rather sickly and hastily made? Are appliquéd areas symmetrical with straight edges or crooked and unbalanced?

Folk arts do not aim at polished perfection, however, and individual variations and irregularities in many cases can add to the charm of the pieces. In the end, thus, you should choose what appeals to you most. Some of my favorites are listed below:

- yellow, double–headed tiger pillows with lively embroidery and appliqué designs
- tiger slippers of black and red with hand–quilted soles and padded uppers

- appliquéd vests or embroidered bibs for children decorated with the five poisonous creatures
- colorfully painted Fengxiang horses or cows

Recommended Stores ★

1. **Qian County Arts and Crafts Factory** ★
   Qian County
   Telephone: inquire through Xian long distance operator

   乾县工艺美术厂门市部
   乾县

   Hours: 9–5

   Accepts traveler's checks and major credit cards

   Has English–speaking staff

   Recommended Crafts

- proud horses with arching necks (25–150 *yuan*)
- camels carrying bearded foreign merchants
- court ladies fashionably plump in the style of the imperial concubine Yang Guifei, with flowing skirts and high coiffures (40–100 *yuan*)

The Qian County Arts and Crafts Factory specializes in re–creations of the vivid, polychrome glazed Tang figures known as *Tang sancai*. These realistic ceramics depict camels carrying sheep, chickens, and silks in their packs, elegantly haughty court ladies, proud horses with arched necks, fearsome tomb guardians, and foreign travelers modeled in a style verging on caricature, all of which provide a delightful view of cosmpolitan life in China during the Tang Dynasty (618–907). Tang protocol determined the quantity and size of such funerary wares, depending upon the deceased's rank as prince, prime minister, or official. According to the customs of the time, burial objects were displayed in the dead man's home and then exhibited as part of the funeral cortege in order to make a dazzling display of the wealth and status of the departed. In the prosperous times of the early Tang Dynasty, funerals became increasingly lavish, and the art of making funerary wares reached its zenith.

Today one of the highlights of a visit to the the Qian County Arts and Crafts Factory is to see the process of reproducing these colorful figures, which includes pouring the mold, sculpting individual details, firing the unglazed ware, applying glaze, and giving the objects a final firing. The distinctive feature of this type of ceramic is that the liquid glazes are deliberately applied in such a way that they drip and flow together in uneven patterns. The resultant pieces, with intense colors of brown, yellow, green, and sometimes blue, capture all the vitality of the Tang originals. This factory produces over 90 different *Tang sancai* figures, of which some of the most striking are court ladies, musicians, foreign merchants, grooms, horses, and camels.

Note: Similar figures are also available at another workshop, the Xian Art Porcelain Factory (telephone: 39942), in the city's east suburbs. A friendly staff here will arrange factory tours and purchases from the adjacent retail shop.

2. Retail Stores at the Museum of the Qin Terra Cotta Army ★
Lintong County
Telephone: 21250

秦始皇兵马俑博物馆外宾服务部
秦始皇兵马俑博物馆

Hours: 8:00–5:45 daily

Cash only

No English–speaking staff

Recommended Crafts

- terra cotta horse heads (30–40 *yuan*)
- full figures of horses from 12" to 18" high (130–300 *yuan*)
- small bronze soldiers (32 *yuan*)
- rubbings in the style of the clay figures (6–20 *yuan*)

One of the most impressive sights in China is the Qin Emperor's army of life–size, realistically sculpted terra cotta archers, foot soldiers, cavalry, and officers fully clad in armor and accompanied by proud war horses and battle chariots. Facing the east in battle array, the silent warriors guard the entrance to the tomb of the mighty First Emperor of the Qin Dynasty. Each figure is molded with individual facial expressions, hair details, and armor, and different regional and racial features are clearly evident. Originally the figures were brightly painted, but the colors have disappeared over the centuries.

A wide variety of reproductions of these terra cotta figures is available for sale at the shops in the museum complex. Vigorous terra cotta horse heads (30–40 *yuan*) and full figures of horses from 12" to 18" (130–300 *yuan*) are among the most impressive pieces here. You can also find a variety of brightly painted warriors which have been re-created in their original colorful style. In addition to clay, there are reproductions in wood, stone, bronze, and paper. There are fine 6" bronze soldiers for 32 *yuan* and carved wooden figures for 80 *yuan*. Eight–inch carved stone horses are 55 *yuan*, while modern rubbings made in the style of the original pieces are available for 6 to 20 *yuan*. And if these prices seem too high, you can always take a look at the free market wares outside the museum entrance.

Since photography inside the exhibition area is forbidden, you may want to consider buying some of the books, postcards, or slides which are sold here. You may not be able to find a similar selection elsewhere.

3. Jade Carving Factory ★
173 Xiyi Street (West First Street)
Telephone: 22085

玉雕厂门市部
西一路173 号

Hours: 9–5

Accepts cash only

Has English–speaking staff

Recommended Crafts

- rubbings of various styles of calligraphy, from single large characters to long inscriptions
- rubbings of paintings with delicate bamboos and orchids

- rubbings with realistic scenes of daily life, made from Han
  Dynasty tiles and bricks

At the Xian Jade Carving Factory visitors can tour the workshops where craftsmen fashion jewelry and small sculptures out of a variety of semi–precious stones and petrified wood. Even more interesting, however, is the workshop where stone rubbings are made. Here one can watch the painstaking process in which a craftsman applies paper to an engraved stone base and then firmly taps ink onto the paper with a special tamper made of cloth tightly wrapped around a fabric center. The preferred material for these rubbings is the thin but highly absorbent paper known as *xuan* paper (named after Xuancheng County in Anhui Province, which is the traditional center for production of this paper). Made primarily of sandalwood tree bark, *xuan* paper is durable yet fine, and its absorbency makes it especially suited for rubbings. This paper was developed by the Tang dynasty, and contributed to the wide popularity and distribution of rubbings during that period.

The rubbings made here are taken from stones which have been carved to duplicate the most important of the inscribed stone tablets in the collection known as the Forest of Stelae at the Shaanxi Provincial Museum. It has been a tradition in China to inscribe model works by great philosophers, painters, and calligraphers on stone so that they will be preserved for posterity and can be copied in rubbings. Some of the original stones in the Forest of Stelae are almost 2,000 years old and are too precious for any more impressions to be made directly. So new stones have been carved to make rubbings. You may, for example, find graceful rubbings of pictures of bamboos and orchids perfectly balanced by lines of fluid calligraphy describing the occasion on which the original painting was done. You may also find bold, eccentric characters written in the style known as "mad grass calligraphy," which looks strikingly similar to works by contemporary expressionist artists in the West.

The retail shops at the Shaanxi Provincial Museum also stock rubbings made from tablets in the Forest of Stelae, but stock is rather limited and variable. You may come across some unusual rubbings made from Moslem tablets at the Mosque in Xian. The retail shop there carries a limited selection of such rubbings.

After buying rubbings, you may be uncertain about how to prepare them for framing, because the paper is often creased. To remove such creases, unfold the rubbing and place it face down on an ironing board with a clean sheet of white paper between the board and the rubbing. Moisten the creased areas with a cloth which has been slightly dampened. Do not apply too much water. Then gently iron the creased areas with a dry iron set at its lowest heat setting. This should remove most of the creases. If at all possible, it is better not to iron the parts of the rubbing that have designs, but to work only on white areas. After being flattened and secured behind glass, most of the creases should not show anyway.

Unless they are made from rarely used old stone tablets, the rubbings are generally inexpensive, ranging from about 3 to 30 *yuan*.

4. Beixiangge (Pavilion of Recorded Good Fortune) ★

Sanxue Road, directly outside the Shaanxi Provincial Museum
Telephone: None

碑祥阁，三学丁，在陕西
博物馆的对面

Hours: 8–5:45 daily

Accepts cash only

No English–speaking staff

Recommended Crafts

- small carved pendants in a variety of stones (5–40 *yuan*)
- carved seeds tied with silk cords

A stop in this store may be enjoyable for those particularly interested in jewelry and small stone carvings. The staff here is quite helpful and pleasant. The store has unusual carved pieces of agate with water drops trapped within the stone, as well as a large selection of carved pendants in a variety of stones for 5 to 40 *yuan*. An unusual item here is a pendant carved from a large, flat seed with a natural fragrance. Tied with silk cords, the pendant is quite decorative.

5. Retail Shop at the Satellite Tombs of Princess Yongtai and Prince Zhanghuai near Qian Ling ★

Telephone: Inquire through Xian long distance operator

永泰公主和章怀太子墓外宾服务部
乾陵

Hours: variable; check in advance

Accepts cash only

No English–speaking staff

Recommended Crafts

- silk embroidered bridal slippers with appliquéd designs on the bottom of the sole (12–20 *yuan*)
- handmade, colorfully cross–stitched insoles (3–8 *yuan*)

Near Qian Ling, the mausoleum of the third Tang Emperor Gaozong and his empress, Wu Zetian, are located seventeen satellite tombs of officials and members of the imperial family. Five of these tombs have been excavated since 1960, yielding realistic mural paintings, stone engravings, and a vast array of polychrome glazed pottery. Visitors to the tombs of Princess Yongtai and Prince Zhanghuai may want to look in at the small commune store across the courtyard from the exhibition area. On past visits we have found selected reproductions of Tang polychrome ceramics and locally made fabric toys. Most interesting, however, are the pastel silk wedding slippers with colorful silk appliqués of birds and flowers on the bottoms of the soles. Decorated with auspicious symbols such as the lotus, peony, butterfly, and magpie, the shoes represent a hope that the bride and groom be prosperous, healthy, and grow together into old age. You may also find colorfully cross–stitched insoles, which are a local traditional craft. It is the custom in this area for a bride to make these insoles as a gift for her husband.

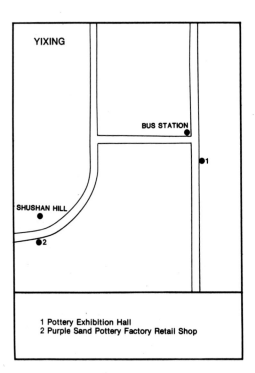

YIXING

BUS STATION

SHUSHAN HILL

1 Pottery Exhibition Hall
2 Purple Sand Pottery Factory Retail Shop

Yixing

Nestled west of Lake Tai, amid scenic streams and canals, rustling forests of bamboo, and mist–covered slopes dense with tea shrubs, Yixing County has for centuries been known as the pottery capital of China. Its location provides all the requirements for superior pottery: fine clays and abundant fuel to fire them. The hills southeast of Yixing are well endowed with a special clay known as zi–sha or purple sand clay. Although Yixing's characteristic wares are called "purple sand" pottery, other colors of local clay are also used, including tan, yellow, brown, red, black, and gray. Tea lovers prize teapots from Yixing because of the special properties which the iron–rich clay imparts to the pots. Because of their low conductivity, the local clays make vessels which retain heat well. Such teapots will not crack if subjected to sudden, sharp changes of temperature, and can hold tea leaves overnight without losing the fresh flavor. It is even said that after much use, an Yixing pot will produce a rich tasting drink with the addition of boiling water alone. The pots acquire a rich patina with age and should never be washed with soap; a simple rinse with cold water is adequate.

During the Tang Dynasty the popularity of tea drinking spread throughout China, bringing with it a demand for exquisite tea utensils. The preparation of tea now became a serious hobby for scholars and monks, who valued the beverage for its gentle stimulation and association with the pleasures of time spent with congenial companions. Educated gentlemen took a formal approach to the preparation and consumption of tea. Certain ceramic wares were most valued for their enhancement of the color and flavor of tea. Green wares were ranked the highest by the eighth century writer Lu Yu, who wrote the *Classic of*

Tea, an important work which set standards of taste for centuries. The development of celadons and porcelain brought new Chinese wares to accommodate the overwhelming enthusiasm for tea, but by the Ming Dynasty, Yixing stoneware teapots, small and realistically sculpted in the shape of plants, flowers, or tree branches, were considered without equal.

Today a visitor to Dingshuzhen, the major town producing ceramics in Yixing County, will see pottery everywhere. Factories make everything from daily–use pickling jars and steamer pots to colorful ceramic trash bins, garden sets, glazed roof tiles, and building materials. Glazed figurines, wall plaques and dinner services have also entered the local repertoire, although it is still the "purple sand" teapots which are most highly prized.

What to Look For

Yixing's specialty is unglazed stoneware teapots made from the distinctive, iron–rich local clay which turns purplish–red or brown after firing. The teapots have traditionally been most prized because of their heat and flavor–retaining properties. But you will also find a variety of other pottery items, many designed for the scholar's studio, including brush jars, brush rests, water jars, wrist rests, containers for miniature landscapes and dwarf trees, snuff bottles, and clay reproductions of antique bronze vessels. The pottery factories also make small figures and wall plaques.

You may choose any shape or size of teapot—square, round, rectangular or cylindrical. Many are modelled upon the shapes of trees, such as jointed bamboo, weathered pine or gnarled plum. Others take the shape of fruit or gourds, including Buddha's–hand citron, peaches, melons and pumpkins. Before you make your purchase, check that the lid of the pot fits securely and totally covers the opening. If possible, it is also a good idea to check the spout by pouring water from the pot.

Where to Look

It is hard to go anywhere in Dingshuzhen and not see pottery being made, sold, or transported. Even some of the sheds and work areas are constructed of pottery shards. The Pottery Exhibition Hall is downtown near the bus station, across the street from a figurine factory which sells plaques and figurines in a variety of bright glazes. It is a short walk through town along the canal to the Purple Sand Pottery Factory. There are a number of shops in Dingshuzhen which sell local pottery, but you may find the selection better at the retail shops described below.

Highly Recommended Stores ★ ★

1. **Pottery Exhibition Hall** ★ ★
   Yixing County, Dingshuzhen
   (No street address is available; the hall is located in the center of town near the bus station.)
   Telephone: 411

   陶瓷公司陈列馆
   宜兴县丁蜀镇

   Hours: 7–10:30 a.m. and 1–5 p.m. daily

   Accepts cash only

   Has English–speaking staff

   Recommended Crafts

   - reproductions of antique teapots in the exhibition, such as a pot modeled as a branch of flowering plum (40 *yuan*) and a square teapot with a lion crouching on the lid (25 *yuan*).

   When you arrive in Dingshuzhen it will probably be most interesting and helpful to visit the Pottery Exhibition Hall first. Here you can get a sense of the tradition of Yixing pottery, through its flowering during the Ming and Qing Dynasties in brilliant creations produced by the collaboration of artists and potters, and finally to the work of modern craftspeople, of whom a majority are women. Here you will see how ingenious artists have used clay and knife to create objects which are unforgettable in their simplicity and imagination.

   A small teapot takes the shape of a pumpkin, with handles sculpted as a vine and tendrils, the lid as the crown of the pumpkin and a section of stalk, while the spout appears as a curled, worm–eaten leaf. Another teapot seems to be hewn from the bough of a flowering plum tree, with spout, lid and handle wrought as gnarled branches, and the body of the pot scattered with plum blossoms carved in relief. Another pot is modelled upon a section of weathered pine, its body rough with bark, while spout, handle and lid appear as small, twisted twigs. In a nearby case a teapot seems to be captured at the moment of transformation, as clay gives way to grape vines and leaves beneath which a tiny squirrel hides to nibble on tender young fruit. Each of these pots reveals the potters' sensitivity for nature and a desire to incorporate natural patterns and living creatures into the designs.

The exhibition hall also sells selected reproductions of items in its collection. On a recent visit we saw a small teapot with the shape of a bough of flowering plum, and an elegant square teapot on whose lid crouched a tiny lion. The retail shop also carries a variety of figurines and vases made of "purple sand" clay. In addition, pieces from the exhibition collection can be commissioned by special arrangement, although this may require a substantial order.

2. Yixing Purple Sand Pottery Factory Retail Shop ★ ★
Yixing County, Dingshuzhen
Telephone: 424, 244, and 119

紫砂工艺陶瓷厂门市部
宜兴县丁蜀镇

Manager: Li Changhong

Hours: 8:30–11 a.m. and 1–5:30 p.m., closed Sunday

Accepts cash only

Staff speaks limited English

Recommended Crafts

• reproductions of Ming Dynasty teapots shaped as pumpkins, melons or branches of flowering plum

- teapots with witty designs in which frogs, insects, dragons or squirrels are sculpted within a natural setting of branches, tree leaves, or flowers.

After a visit to the Pottery Exhibition Hall, take a tour of the Yixing Purple Sand Pottery Factory to see how pieces are produced today. Here potters cast teapots using one or more molds for the body of the pot. Spouts and handles are cast separately and then joined to the body, after which a wet brush is used to smooth out any irregularities in the joining. The pottery is decorated in a variety of ways. The most simple teapots have no added surface designs, but take their decoration from elegant shapes. Some are imaginatively modeled as gourds, melons, or pumpkins, while others are square, round, or rectangular. In some pieces, clays of different colors have been mixed together to create a swirling effect of yellow, black or brown.

You can see workers with knives carving designs lightly into the teapots while the clay is still soft. Many fine teapots are decorated with a line of poetry flowing beautifully over the surface of the body. A characteristic of Yixing teapots is the use of the seal mark with the name of the potter stamped in intaglio on the clay, something very seldom seen on other Chinese crafts. But it is the sculptural quality of Yixing stoneware which always stands out, whether expressed in the simplest, most restrained shapes or in exuberant, naturalistic fruits or flowers.

At the retail shop of the pottery factory you will find an extensive selection of unglazed Yixing teapots, as well as other objects, such as wine sets, steamer pots, brush rests, and vases made out of the purplish–brown local clay. You may also be interested in the stoneware reproductions of ancient Shang and Zhou Dynasty bronze ritual vessels. Some simple objects may be very inexpensive, less than one *yuan* apiece, while others with complicated details may be priced in the hundreds of *yuan*. The most prized Yixing wares have always been the teapots, and almost every pot made here has its own attractive style. Some of my favorites are a set of teapot and cups shaped as if from a hollow trunk of gnarled flowering plum, with twigs for handles and spout. Some of the pieces, such as the gourd and pumpkin–shaped teapots, have a streamlined elegance which looks strikingly modern. Others show a fresh, witty touch in depicting a frog perched on a gnarled tree branch or a squirrel hidden amid grape leaves. Prices for most of these teapots range from 2 to 50 *yuan*.

Yi minority woman in traditional costume (Beijing chapter)

Cinnabar lacquer bowl (Beijing chapter)

Painted wood and paper
lantern (Beijing chapter)

Mr. Lin Chunxin (Beijing chapter)

Dough figures (Beijing chapter)   Dough figures (Beijing chapter)

Woodblock print of painting by Wu Zuoren (Beijing chapter)

Blanc–de–Chine porcelain pillow (Beijing chapter)

Miao embroidered dragon (Beijing chapter)

Eggshell porcelain from Jingdezhen (Beijing chapter)

Batik clothing (Beijing chapter)

Brocade box (Beijing chapter)

Paper kites from Beijing (Beijing chapter)

Making porcelain garden seat (Beijing chapter)

Folk–print textiles (Beijing chapter)

Sichuan embroidery (Chengdu chapter)

Wood carving of scene from classical novel *The Water Margin*
(Beijing chapter)

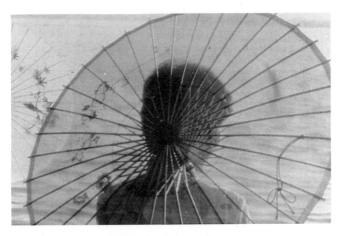

Embroidered soles for cloth shoes (Chengdu chapter)

Painted silk umbrella (Fuzhou chapter)

Guangzhou embroidery of peonies (Guangzhou and Foshan chapter)

Blue–and–white underglaze porcelain (Guangzhou and Foshan chapter)

Ivory spheres within ivory spheres (Guangzhou and Foshan chapter)

Foshan papercut (Guangzhou and Foshan chapter)

Zhejiang woven bamboo rooster (Hangzhou chapter)

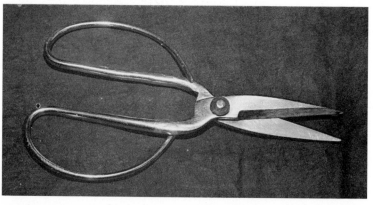

Scissors used for embroidery and papercutting (Hangzhou chapter)

Carpet weaving in Lhasa (Lhasa chapter)

Bride in traditional Tibetan costume (Lhasa chapter)

Reproduction of an antique celadon ram (Nanjing chapter)

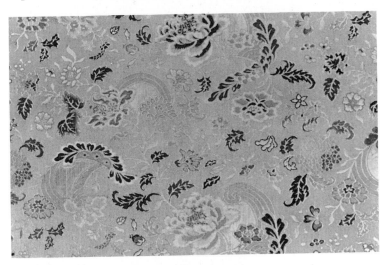

Brocade with flower motifs (Nanjing chapter)

Reproductions of Tang dynasty Polychrome glazed ceramics
(Shanghai chapter)

Harvest time, Jinshan County peasant painting (Shanghai chapter)

Neighborhood fireworks, Jinshan County peasant painting
(Shanghai chapter)

Interior painted snuff bottles (Shanghai chapter)

Dehua *blanc–de–Chine*
porcelain figure
(Shanghai chapter)

Carved sandalwood fan (Suzhou chapter)

Suzhou embroiderers at work (Suzhou chapter)

Double–sided embroidery on silk (Suzhou chapter)

New Year print (Tianjin chapter)

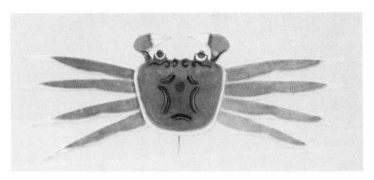

Tianjin kite (Tianjin chapter)

Tiger shoes (Xian chapter)

Neolithic pot from Banpo Village (Xian chapter)

Shadow figure (Xian chapter)

Shadow figure (Xian chapter)

"Fragrant pouches" (Xian chapter)

Yixing potter at work (Yixing chapter)

Craft Terms and Techniques

Jade and Ivory Carving

To the ancient Chinese, jade was the most precious of stones, the symbol of all virtue, whose magical qualities made it more valuable than gold or silver. Jade was accorded immense value because of its physical properties—indestructibility, luster, and resonance—which were associated with the human attributes of wisdom, purity, moral courage, power, and immortality. The pre–eminent position of jade is reflected in the art and literature of China from its earliest history down through the centuries even to the present. Ancient philosophers spoke of its pure and moral influences, while alchemists, fascinated by the stone's strength, tried to find ways to transmute its power. The consumption of jade was reputed to make one pure and indestructible, spurring ancient emperors to drink a mix of powdered jade and water in an attempt to become immortal. Early kings carried jade scepters as emblems of authority, while nobles were given discs and other objects of jade as symbols of status and imperial favor.

Over thousands of years, Chinese carvers have mastered the design and execution of objects in jade. Before the chisel or drill is even lifted, the artist must carefully consider the raw stone or block, noting its special qualities, inner patterns, and grain. The design and subject that are selected must be appropriate to these characteristics. The process, almost mystical at times, demands a great experience with the structure and varieties of jade. The best sculpture incorporates the natural designs of the raw mineral, taking streaks of color as integral part of the final design.

The Chinese term for **jade**, *yu*, has traditionally included a number of hard, rare, and beautiful stones, including agate and quartz, but nephrite alone was held to be "true jade" (zhen–yu), which has been prized since neolithic times in China. Another closely related mineral, jadeite, has also been included in the category of jade, but was introduced to China much later, probably in the 18th century.

Nephrite is found in the mountains of Xinjiang Province, from which it has been exported for centuries. Nephrite boulders and pebbles are found in river beds as well as in rock formations worked in mines and quarries. When polished, the stone has an oily luster. Nephrite is cold to the touch, resonant, and translucent when thinly cut. The modern Chinese term for nephrite is *ruanyu*, or "soft jade."

Jadeite is a tough, granular mineral similar in texture and hardness to nephrite. When polished, the stone acquires a brilliant, glassy finish. While nephrite has been prized in China for centuries, jadeite was probably first brought to China in the 18th century from Burma. The modern Chinese term for jadeite is *yingyu*, or "hard jade."

Jadeite and nephrite occur in a broad range of **colors**, including white, yellow, red, indigo blue, gray, and black, as well as the green tones, which are probably the best known. Some of the most precious types of both jadeite and nephrite, called "muttonfat" jade, are pure white. Often veins and flecks of several colors appear on one boulder due to the presence of iron, manganese, chromium, and other elements. The muttonfat variety with vermilion flecks is highly prized, as are stones of spinach green splashed with gold, emerald "kingfisher" jadeite, and stones with veins of green amid pale white known as "moss amid melting snow."

Jade is **shaped** by the use of cutting tools and an abrasive powder. Quartz crystals, crushed garnets, or rubies were used before the discovery of the synthetic carborundum, which is widely used today in China. The grinding effect is due to the slow action of the abrasive paste, rather than to the sharpness of the cutting tools. Large pieces of jade are first rough–cut with a wire saw and abrasive paste. Then various discs and gougers of graduated sizes aid the artist in shaping the progressively finer lines of the work. By these methods a carver with great experience and infinite patience creates intricate and delicate objects, such as a chain of separately moveable but interlocking links cut from a single piece of jade. The final step is polishing by the use of leather buffers with an abrasive paste. This painstaking process produces the sharp lines and smooth surface of the finished object.

A **design** in jade is never created before the jade or hardstone is carefully studied, and every streak or spot of color, every aspect of grain and texture, thoroughly examined. Flaws or imperfections may become a part of the design or may be cleverly cut away. The design is finally the product of the carver's creative vision, which allows him or her to "see" within the stone and "release" the bird, fish, or animal captured there.

Although **ivory** never held the same importance as jade it, too, was a rare imported material in demand among nobles, scholars, and rich merchants as a symbol of status. Derived from elephant tusks, the teeth and horns of whale, walrus, hippopotamus, rhinoceros, and boar, ivory may occur in a variety of tones from purest white to yellow and even brown. The material is valued by carvers for its grain, smooth texture, and rich, natural feel. Ivory can be polished to a high sheen, and fine old pieces have often acquired a special gloss from long handling. Ivory absorbs moisture readily and will crack if exposed to extremes of moisture, dryness, or temperature. A relatively soft material, ivory requires no abrasive for sculpting.

Elephants, which existed in northern China in prehistoric times, were still found there until about the middle of the first millennium BC, and their tusks provided ivory for ornamental objects and vessels inlaid with turquoise stones. Today the ivory for objects sculpted in China comes largely from African elephant tusks.

Styles of ivory carving differ noticeably from region to region. The northern school of ivory carvers, represented by the ivories produced in Beijing during the Ming and Qing Dynasties, is characterized by creative and meticulous craftsmanship. Landscapes and figures are combined in sculptures which incorporate realism with imaginative and decorative elements. The southern style of ivory carving, centered in Guangzhou, is more elaborate and may feature subjects such as the traditional ornate flower boats and the famous multiple concentric balls. During most of the Qing Dynasty, Guangzhou was the center of trade between China and the rest of the world. Generation after generation of ivory and jade carvers worked here, specializing in carving concentric balls, each of which spins freely inside another.

Since jade sculptures may command very high prices, it is especially important to familiarize yourself with types of stones and color varieties before you make any purchase. When shopping for "jade" items in China, one should be aware of the variety of hard and semi--precious stones which the Chinese include in this category: if you are looking only for jadeite, then you must be sure to specify this. Also check sculpted pieces to be sure that lines are clearly and crisply carved and that uncarved surfaces are finely polished. With colored or veined stones, look for sculptures which incorporate the color variations as part of the finished design.

Note: American customs regulations prohibit the importation of ivory from whales, walruses, or any source other than the African elephant; such pieces will be confiscated at the point of entry. American travellers should also be aware that they may only bring back African ivory pieces for their personal use. (Commercial transactions require a special permit.) Thus quantity should be limited to four or five pieces. You should also be aware that the Indian elephant is classed as an endangered species, and products from Indian ivory cannot be brought into the U.S., nor can any rhinoceros horn pieces, for the same reason. Another item to be aware of is black coral, which is a protected item, and can be brought into the U.S. in limited quantities for personal use, but requires a permit for larger, commercial transactions.

Textiles

The origins of silk production are lost in Chinese prehistory, but the discovery of 4,000 year old fragments of silk fabric and thread indicates the age of this craft. The first silk fabrics were made from wild silkworms, but later the worms were domesticated and the production of silk became a major part of China's domestic economy. By the 9th century BC, China had already begun to export silk to the Middle East along the caravan trails of the Silk Road, and silk quickly became the principle medium of trade between China and the rest of the world. Silk production was a jealously guarded Chinese secret. The Romans thought that silk was a type of vegetable fiber, and as long as China alone could provide this gossamer fabric, a thriving trade with the Middle East was assured. It is not surprising, therefore, that taking silkworms out of the country was a crime punishable by death.

Silk is a natural fiber made from the cocoon spun by the larvae of several types of Asian moths, some of which are wild and some of which are domesticated. By a complicated process this protein filament is transformed into fine fabrics. Most commercial silk sold today is made from the domesticated mulberry silkworm, although the rough, slub texture silk made from uncultivated silkworms continues to be a popular variation.

The cultivation of the mulberry silkworm is a laborious process. First the silkworm eggs are carefully incubated, hatching into larvae which gorge themselves constantly for 28 days on fresh mulberry leaves. After this the worms spin their cocoons, taking about three days. The finished cocoons are then washed in water to remove impurities and silk gum. Next several filaments are caught and twisted together to form thread, a process known as reeling. The silk is further bleached and boiled to improve color, softness, and purity.

Variations in the cultivation or processing of the silk may produce markedly different types of fabric. Wild or raw silk is a rough textured fabric made from uncultivated caterpillars fed on oak leaves; this fabric is also called tussah silk, and may be used to make pongee, a nubby silk, and shantung. *Dupion* silk is a slub textured silk which originates from two caterpillars who spin one cocoon, yielding knotted yarns when processed.

The yarn of the cocoon may be processed in three ways. The most elastic, lustrous silk is made when the silk filaments are reeled. The end of the silk filaments is carefully located and then filaments from five or six cocoons are twisted to form thread. Then about seven of these threads are twisted together once again. Another type of silk known as spun silk is made from tangled silk floss which cannot be reeled in one continuous filament. These short or uneven pieces are combed and then pulled through rollers to make them straight and even. The strands must have more twists than reeled silk so that all the short fibers will be tightly held; the extra twisting makes the fabric less lustrous and elastic, however, so that spun silk is not as expensive as reeled silk. The third type of silk, known as silk noil or waste silk, is processed from material left over when making spun silk. This yarn is rather dull, rough, and uneven, but some find its texture to be interesting. It is generally less expensive than other types of silk.

Over the centuries Chinese textile workers have evolved a number of techniques for weaving and decorating silk and other fabrics. Some of the most important types are described below.

The process of **weaving**, which creates fabric by interlacing sets of threads along the length and width of the material, is well documented in China as early as the Neolithic Period. Warp threads running along the length of the fabric and weft threads moving crosswise over and under the warp form the cloth, woven first using simple frames such as squatting looms or waist looms, but later from more complicated treadle looms and, eventually, elaborate jacquard looms. In weaving, thousands of combinations of warp and weft thread are possible, providing an endless variety of patterns.

For a simple "tabby weave," for example, one weft thread crosses over one warp thread and under the next warp thread, while a brocade fabric may carry a simple tabby weave background set against an elaborate pattern of birds and flowers in a contrasting weave. Another type of woven tapestry is called *ke–si* or "cut silk." These exquisite creations reproduce flowers, birds, or landscapes in silk thread. Weavers use a traditional wooden loom, but rather than one single shuttle for the weft thread, they use a number of shuttles, breaking up the weft into segments to create different patterns and colors. Part of the finished effect is the pattern of spaces between the various weft segments, which is visible when the tapestry is held up to the light. Suzhou, Hangzhou, Nanjing, and Chengdu were traditional centers for silk weaving which continue to be important today.

Another technique of fabric decoration is **embroidery**, which is probably almost as old as the production of cloth itself. The earliest Chinese embroidered fabrics were worked with a simple chain stitch. By the Han Dynasty, at least eight stitches were commonly used, while today there are more than forty. Satin stitch, a closely worked straight stitch, produces a smooth, even finish. The stitch slant and length may be varied to create different shading effects. Double–sided embroideries are worked in satin stitch exclusively, with the stitches being mirror images on front and back. Another important Chinese embroidery stitch is the seed stitch or "Peking knot," a tiny ring formed when thread is looped around the needle before each stitch is made. In older fabrics you may frequently find floral designs accentuated by areas of clustered Peking knots. It is said that the stitch was eventually banned because it caused blindness in the needleworkers. Guangdong, Hunan, and Sichuan Provinces are well known for their embroidery styles, while Suzhou needleworkers are famous for their double–sided embroidery.

Other decorative techniques may be seen in Chinese **folk textiles**, which show a great variety of colors and symbols, reflecting the rich local traditions of their place of origin. Over the centuries each village has developed its own particular style, which has been further refined from family to family and daughter to daughter. In addition, each of China's minority nationalities, especially Zhuang, Yao, Miao, and Yi, has particular decorative styles and heritages which have increased the rich diversity of folk textile forms. The most important decorative techniques are embroidery, hand stencil printing, and resist dyeing (including batik).

Like her urban sister, the cotton–clad village woman learned to embroider early in life. Embroidery pattern books became part of a young woman's inheritance, prized by generation after generation. The folk art of papercutting is directly related to peasant embroidery patterns, and both of these arts reached great heights in Zhejiang and Jiangsu provinces in central China, where silk was produced in abundance.

The old dyeing techniques are still used by village women today. Fabrics may be block printed by hand using wooden blocks inked with dye and stamped on the cloth. Another traditional technique is resist dyeing. For patterns women use a waterproof stencil made from oiled paper or parchment. The open areas are covered with wax or a lime and soybean flour mixture, to resist the dye. The cloth is dipped in an indigo bath and then dried. Finally the lime and flour paste is scraped off. The fabric that emerges presents a bold contrast of creamy white and robust indigo, used to make quilt covers, curtains, scarves, clothing, and even to wrap bundles. The minority women of south and southwest China are especially noted for their bold batik pictures, created by applying wax to areas of fabric which are to remain undyed. The cloth is then dyed, dried, and the paraffin removed, leaving a bold contrast of patterns as well as a network of cracks from the wax, which adds a sense of depth and texture to the finished design.

The **symbols** which adorn Chinese textiles convey a rich world of meaning to the viewer who understands their significance. Most imposing and formalized of Chinese textiles are the dragon robes which were worn by the emperor, his relatives, and officials. These ceremonial garments were woven and embroidered with symbols of prosperity and longevity. All of the robes contained dragon designs, which had been associated with imperial power as far back as the Shang Dynasty. Clothed in his ceremonial robes strewn with cosmic symbols, the emperor became identical with the universe itself. The officials who stood before him in turn were clearly ranked by the emblems on their dragon robes, so that these garments became the concrete embodiment of the elaborate Chinese feudal system.

Auspicious symbols constitute another important body of motifs appearing on Chinese textiles. Butterflies, pine trees, chrysanthemums, peaches, deer, and cranes denote longevity, while the tiger in its many manifestations represents strength and courage. The many–seeded pomegranate represents the hope of having many sons, an idea also conveyed by the hundred sons motif showing a lively squad of young boys engaged in all manner of amusements. Floral designs are also popular, with the lotus representing purity and abundance, the peony wealth and honor, and the orchid moral virtue.

Another type of motif originates in plays on words. The phrase for goldfish, *jin yu*, sounds like the phrase "gold in abundance," for example, while red bat or *hong fu* sounds like "profuse good fortune." On some folk textiles you may see a lotus and fish design, which by a play on words conveys the hope that one have "abundance for year after year." In another textile scene a small boy sits on a lotus, carrying a reed pipe and cassia flowers; this design represents the hope that "for generation after generation one may have sons who attain high rank."

When choosing a textile, keep in mind the style of the piece and the use for which it was intended. Folk vests for babies will have a very different look from official garments, for example. Regardless of use, however, textiles should show skillful needlework with regular stitches, even edges, and a majority of handwork. Do not be afraid to look inside pieces to check for spotting, frayed edges, or holes. Although machine made items and items incorporating ricrack and plastic decoration are becoming more numerous in China, it is still possible to find a wide selection of handmade textiles in the traditional style.

Ceramics

Ceramic wares, made of a mixture of clay along with smaller quantities of feldspar and quartz, are shaped when the clay is moist and then hardened by heat. Pottery was China's first art form, and ceramic wares have continued to occupy an important place among Chinese crafts. Down through the centuries Chinese potters have experimented with various mixtures of clay, color, glaze, and shape to bring ceramics to the level of a major art form.

Earthenware is a type of pottery formed of coarse, often unrefined clay mixed with sand (silica) for added strength. After firing in a kiln at a relatively low temperature from 800 to 1000 degrees Centigrade, these wares are thick, porous, brittle, and fairly easily broken. Application of a glaze gives earthenware objects a hard coat which makes them impervious to liquid.

Stoneware is made from clay combined with fusible materials such as feldspar and quartz. Such wares are fired at kiln temperatures from 1100 to 1250 degrees Centigrade, making a strong, hard, non–porous, and well–vitrified finished product.

Glaze is a liquid mixture applied to clay objects. After firing the object develops a glossy coat. Crackle is a pattern which occurs in the glaze as a network of cracks occurring when body and glaze cool at different rates.

Porcelains are hard, nonporous, translucent ceramics made from a highly refined white clay called kaolin mixed in almost equal proportions with a white feldspathic powder called *petuntse* or "China clay." The word kaolin is derived from the location where this type of clay was found in large quantity, in the Gaoling Hills near Jingdezhen, Jiangxi Province. The addition of petuntse to kaolin makes the finished objects less brittle, and proportion varies with the quality of the ceramic—the finer the porcelain, the greater the amount of kaolin used.

Porcelain glazes are made of the same feldspathic composition as the body. After application of the liquid glaze, objects are fired at kiln temperatures of at least 1200 Degrees Centigrade. As this heat, body and glaze fuse and become totally vitrified. The finished wares are translucent, non–porous, and produce a clear ringing sound like metal when struck.

Bodiless or eggshell porcelains are made with extremely thin walls so fine and white that objects can be clearly seen through the porcelain object when held up to light.

Bisque or biscuit refers to a ceramic which is fired without a glaze at temperatures from about 800 to 1300 Degrees Centigrade. The biscuit may then be glazed or decorated with enamels which require a lower firing temperature. In figurines such as those produced at Shiwan in Guangdong Province, the faces and flesh areas are left unglazed for a realistic effect and to accentuate the detailed modeling of the features, while the rest of the figure is painted with glossy enamels. After painting, such figures are refired.

Slip is a thin mixture of liquid clay applied to correct defects in color or shape or to provide a base for painted decoration. Separate parts, such as the spout and handles of a teapot, may be joined to the clay body by means of a slip.

Dotted over the landscape of South China are traditional "**dragon kilns**," built in tunnels up the hillside with each chamber higher than the one connected below. Some had as many as ten or twelve chambers which fired ceramics at different temperatures. Most kilns used today in China are computerized and transport objects through at a continuous, even rate, but for certain effects the old dragon kilns must still be used.

Underglaze painting is a technique in which the artist paints designs directly onto an unfired porcelain body, applies a thin coat of clear glaze, and then fires the ceramic. The finished design appears to float between the glaze and body. From the Ming Dynasty, blue–and–white underglaze porcelains have an been extremely popular ceramic form and continue to be produced today. Underglaze red wares are also a distinctive and popular type of Chinese ceramics.

Overglaze painting is a technique in which enamel colors are applied to a glazed and fired porcelain object, which is then refired. The famous "famille verte" and "famille rose" wares so popular in the Qing Dynasty required the use of special translucent enamels, and were made by this method.

Rice grain pattern is a popular type of ceramic decoration in which small holes are pierced in the unfired clay body of an object, originally by using grains of rice. After underglaze painting is applied, the object is glazed and fired. Glaze fills the perforations and forms a pattern of translucent patches which is clearly seen when the object is held up to light.

Ceramic funerary wares were created to be buried in a tomb for use by the dead in the afterlife. These clay burial figures were modelled by hand or made in molds, then painted and finished individually after firing. In the 1st through 3rd centuries BC, these figures were in such demand that imperial workshops in the capital and provinces began mass production to meet the demand. The ceramics buried in Han tombs reflect the whole range of furnishings and implements actually used in the homes of the wealthy upper classes of that period, from multi–storied houses to farms and pigsties, from elegant ladies and lively musicians to dogs, bears, and galloping horses. The artisan's goal was to create objects so lifelike that they would continue to exist in the afterworld much as they existed in life.

Tang polychrome glazed burial figures (*Tang sancai*), fashioned with realistic detail and vivid colors, depict camels carrying sheep, chickens, and silks in their packs, elegantly haughty court ladies, proud horses with arched necks, fearsome tomb guardians, and foreign travelers modelled in a style verging on caricature provide a delightful view of cosmopolitan Tang life. Tang protocol determined the quantity and size of such funerary wares, depending upon the deceased's rank as prince, prime minister, or official. According to the customs of the time, burial objects were displayed in the dead person's home and then exhibited as part of the funeral cortege in order to make a dazzling display of the wealth and status of the departed. In Xian, Luoyang, and other ancient cities where ceramic workshops existed centuries ago, modern ceramic artists are meticulously re–creating these fine old figures using a combination of traditional techniques and modern tools.

Blanc–de–chine or "ivory" porcelain figures have been a traditional specialty of the city of Dehua in Fujian Province for several centuries. These sculptures of Buddha, Guan–yin (the Buddhist Goddess of Mercy), and other religious and legendary figures were usually pure white, carved with fluid lines and careful detail beneath a thick, creamy glaze.

Cizhou wares are robust stonewares from Handan, Hebei Province decorated by bold designs which are carved through a black or brown glaze to a white slip or sketched on white or cream slip using a quick, freehand painting style. The pieces are then coated with a clear glaze and high–fired. Popular designs on Cizhou ware include animals, insects, flowers, fat babies, and little boys at play. These bold ceramics were made from the 10th century for the use of the common people of north China, and today their production has been revived.

Celadons, perhaps the loveliest and best known among Chinese ceramics, derive their distinct green, gray–green, or olive colors from iron–tinged glazes. The Chinese prize celadons for their color, which was said to resemble "the tones of distant hills," "the soft jade–green of onion sprouts in autumn," "a wet, mossy bank," or "slender willow twigs." Celadons resemble precious jade in luster and tone, and it is probable that early Daoist alchemists were searching for ways to create artificial jade when celadons were first produced. Today kilns in Longguan, Zhejiang Province and Yaozhou and Xian in Shaanxi Province produce fine celadon vases, bowls, and plates with traditional incised or impressed designs in low relief beneath a thick, smooth, shiny glaze of soft olive or gray–green. Crackle glazes are also sometimes used for additional decoration.

Popular **symbols** on Chinese pottery and porcelain include the ever–present dragon in his many manifestations, five auspicious red bats, the "three friends" of prunus, pine, and bamboo, floral designs of peony, lotus or plum blossoms, chubby baby boys, deer and peaches denoting longevity, and fish to represent abundance. The array of motifs seen on painted ceramics includes the entire repertoire of symbols common to all the arts of China. Over the centuries these designs have been copied from other crafts and fine arts but interpreted time and time again with new life and individual style.

When looking at the somewhat daunting variety of Chinese ceramics, watch for basic imperfections such as pitting, uneven glazing, and cracks. Classically simple shapes and luminous, even glazes continue to distinguish well made ceramics, while you may expect reproductions of funerary figures to be more robust, colorful and realistic. Folk ceramics may have some irregularities in glaze or form, but this need not mar their charm, which lies in their distinctive shapes, freedom of painted decoration and realistic representation.

Lacquerware

Lacquer painting, as well as the crafting of beautiful, light and graceful vessels in lacquer, was already an accomplished Chinese art over two thousand years ago. The lac tree is native to China and grows wild over the south and central areas. When the unique preservative properties of the sap of the tree were discovered, it was quickly used to coat boat, food utensils, weapons, and leather. Artisans found that the glossy substance could be colored and dried to a hard, shiny surface, excellent for decoration. In fact, the best record of early styles of painting comes from thousands of pieces of painted lacquerware which have been found perfectly preserved after being buried over two thousand years ago.

Lacquer comes from the sap of the lac tree, *Rhus verniciflua*, a variety of sumac. On contact with air the sap hardens, producing a coat which is resistant to corrosion, rust, acids, insects, and moisture, thus protecting against disintegration and chemical change. The raw lacquer, or lac, is collected and purified, forming a shiny, transparent liquid. Mineral pigments supply the colors, which are added before the lacquer is sealed in airtight containers. Black and red—from iron and mercury, respectively—are the two most important colors of lacquerware. Traditionally red was used for carving and black as a base for painting.

The **base** may be either wood, leather, or copper. Wood is carefully primed and polished and then covered with a silk or hempen cloth which has been soaked in raw lacquer. A copper base is usually finished with enamel.

Lacquerware is **formed** by building up successive layers of lac. Each coat must dry thoroughly in a moist, temperature–controlled, dust–free, atmosphere. A piece may require over one hundred coats of lacquer before being ready for carving; fewer coats are required for incising or painting. Each layer is ground and polished before the next coat is applied; the final layer is polished a smooth, mirror–like finish ready for final decoration.

Lacquer carving was developed as early as the Tang Dynasty and has been a specialty of Beijing's lacquerware workshops. Between 100 and 200 coats of lacquer may be needed, depending on the depth required for the design; at least half–inch walls are usually needed. The elaborately and intricately carved objects traditionally associated with Beijing workshops are of a red color known as cinnabar, made by adding mercuric sulfide to the lac. Some carved wares have several colors in successive layers, carved at different depths to reveal the various colors. Open–work effects are also popular, as are high and low relief carving.

Lacquer–based paints are used to sketch traditional motifs such as landscapes, flowers, and animals, usually on a black background. A fine gold outline may frame the painted design, while a thin coat of transparent lacquer provides the final touch. Chongqing and Chengdu in Sichuan Province were both traditional centers for painted lacquer and continue to be important today.

Incising is another popular lacquer technique. After incising, the pattern lines are filled with silver or gold, or another lacquer color. Many decorative techniques, such as painting, incising, carving, and inlay, are combined in contemporary lacquer designs.

Lacquer inlay may also be used to decorate lacquerware objects. Gold, silver, coral, jade, ivory, and mother–of–pearl are shaped into mosaics of landscapes, flowers, and animals against a background of black lacquer. Always designed with careful regard for their natural colors, these lacquer inlays are an especially popular decoration in screens, cabinets, and other pieces of furniture. They are a specialty of Yangzhou, in Jiangsu Province, which also uses the inlay technique for exquisite small plates and trays.

Bodiless lacquer is extremely lightweight, formed of successive layers of lacquer applied to a cloth–covered base, which is removed after the layers have dried. In the Tang Dynasty the technique was used to create fluid statues of Buddhist deities. Such images were first modeled in clay, and then numerous coats of liquid lacquer were added, exactly reproducing the form of the original sculpture. When the lacquer had dried the clay was removed, leaving a light yet durable figure. Today in the city of Fuzhou, Fujian Province, there are two lacquerware factories with over one thousand workers who specialize in making bodiless lacquerware screens, vases, trays, and other objects.

During the 18th century, screens became a popular export item from China. Carved screens of lacquer were especially popular, and those made for export were often rather roughly fashioned in Fuzhou or Guangzhou. Instead of using the expensive and time–consuming method of building up hundreds of layers of lacquer, artisans applied a relatively small number of lacquer coats to a wooden base. The carving style was bold and the exposed areas of the wooden base were given a coat of brightly colored lacquer paint. The resultant pieces were called "**coromandel**" **screens** because they were shipped from China to the Coromandel Coast of southwest India and from there to Europe and the West.

A variety of **symbols and decoration** can be found on lacquerware. Painted items are often decorated in the style of the Warring States Period and early Han Dynasty: red and black lacquerware painted with graceful designs of fighting dragons and dancing birds which dissolve into a background of abstract spirals. Other reproductions are decorated with cloud designs and mythical animals. On the carved cinnabar lacquerware of Beijing you may find detailed landscape scenes or floral patterns, while inlaid screens display bustling genre scenes or bird and flower designs. Bodiless lacquer may imitate almost any type of ceramic or bronze. Some have painted designs covered by coats of lacquer so that the pattern is only faintly visible, as, for example, in a tray where luminous goldfish appear to glide in deep waters.

When selecting painted lacquer or bodiless lacquerware items, be sure that all surfaces are smoothly finished to a high sheen with no pitting or cracks. Check inlaid items to be sure the mosaics are evenly finished and securely attached. Choose lacquer furniture which has fittings which close firmly and shelves which slide easily; avoid those with uneven or warped edges. Objects of carved lacquer should have sharp, clearly delineated lines, precision in small details, and smooth, polished finishes on uncarved surfaces. Look for items with a variety of patterns combining openwork along with low and high relief.

Cloisonné and Metalwork

The art of enameling originated as a substitute form of inlay: instead of using precious and semi–precious stones, bright and colorful enamels were inlaid into gold ornaments. From the beginning, workers in cloisonné required the patronage of the court or the very rich, as the craft required precious materials and involved a highly technical process of production. In fact almost all cloisonné was made in Beijing, which is the home of China's most important cloisonné workshops today.

The **enameling** process joins glass to metal, two substances of very different physical properties. Unlike ceramic glazes, an enamel surface does not fuse with its metal base, but only adheres to it. Thus the artisan must exercise great skill in order to join these two disparate elements.

Cloisonné wares are made of closed cells or partitions formed of thin wires of bronze or copper. The wire *cloisons* (partitions) are filled with enamel paste and may vary in shape depending on the design. They are formed in intricate patterns and attached by adhesive to a copper base. The wires are then permanently fused to the base by solder, which is dusted over the surface. The *cloisons* are filled with colored enamel pastes and fired after the enamel has dried. As the enamels contract in firing, several fillings and firings may be necessary to produce the final, even surface. After firing, the surface is polished with powdered charcoal and the copper wires are gilded by electroplate, which adds radiance to the final design.

The metal **base** of cloisonné objects may take many shapes, including vases, jewelry, covered boxes, tea sets, bowls, or animal forms such as cranes, dragons, camels, or horses.

The two distinctive **cloisonné colors** have traditionally been turquoise and cobalt blue, which were enhanced by richly decorative gilt outlines. Today new enamel shades increase the subtlety of available colors, and reproductions of classic paintings are now executed in cloisonné.

Painted **enamelware** objects are formed of a layer of opaque enamel, often white, applied to a metal base. A design is painted on with additional coats of colored enamel and then the piece is fired. The technique was developed initially at Limoges in France and was probably imported to China in the early 18th century. Chinese painted enamels were a specially of Guangzhou (Canton) and were thus termed "Canton enamels."The bulk of this work was commissioned by Western merchants for export; European motifs, religious scenes, and emblems such as coats of arms were popular designs. Today teapots, covered boxes, smoking sets, and plates are made by this method, but their popularity has never approached that of cloisonné in China.

Reproductions of ancient **bronzes** also continue to be popular Chinese craft items. Made by ancient techniques developed over 4,000 years ago, these vessels were used in ritual sacrifices to commemorate important military victories. The early pieces are stylized and rather awesome, with mystical animal masks, plumed birds, coiling dragons, and other zoomorphic motifs set amid thunder patterns. Later bronzes were decorated with fluid cloud spirals and streamlined geometric patterns, all superbly enhanced by inlays of silver, gold, turquoise, and malachite.

Chinese metalwork and filigree techniques are also used to create silver and gold **jewelry**. In the fifth century Chinese silver and goldsmiths began to adapt designs imported from the Middle East via the Silk Road. Later gold ornaments and jewelry made extensive use of filigree and inlays of semi–precious stones. During the Qing Dynasty Manchu noblewomen wore elaborate headdresses of gilded silver filigree on a metal foundation inset with semi–precious stones. Brilliant blue–green kingfisher feathers added a final touch of opulence. Ornate headdresses of kingfisher feathers and gilded silver filigree also formed part of the official costume of the Qing Dynasty emperors. Today Beijing is once again the center of the work in rare metals, jewelry, and semi–precious stones. Craft workers create fantastic dragons, phoenixes, horses and human figures of solid gold or gold and silver filigree inset with coral, amethyst, pearls, rubies, and turquoise. Beijing is also renowned for its fine gold and silver jewelry encrusted with polished semi–precious stones set in **Cabochon**, or unfaceted, style.

When selecting jewelry, it is wise to check the settings and closings carefully, as these parts may not be very durable. If you find a stone or setting which you like, it may even be advisable to have the settings replaced when you return home.

Glossary

Note: although many sounds of spoken Chinese are not used by English speakers, the following chart of sounds and tones may help you in pronouncing the Chinese terms used in this glossary. Words are spelled in the *pinyin* romanization system presently used in China and by most Western publications.

To pronounce a word properly, you will also have to pay attention to its tone, one of four pitches which will change the word's meaning. When pronounced in the low third tone, for example, the word *mai* means "buy," but pronounced in the falling fourth tone *mai* means "sell."

Approximate Pronunciation Guide for Chinese Sounds

pinyin Chinese	*English*
a	as in father
an	as in con
ao	as in now
b	as in big
c	as in cheap
d	as in dog
e	as in book
ei	as in eight
f	as in frog
g	as in game, but strongly aspirated
h	as in home, but strongly aspirated

pinyin Chinese	English
i	as in sir (when preceded by z, c, s, zh, ch, sh, and r); otherwise as in machine
ian	as ye in yen
j	as in jeep
k	as in king, but strongly aspirated
l	as in lamb
m	as in mug
n	as in name
o	as in paw
ou	as in boat
p	as in pig
q	as in cheap
r	as in French *je*
s	as in single
sh	as in shrimp
t	as in tip
u	as in dune
u	as in French *tu*
ua	as wha in what
w	as in way
x	as in sheep
y	as in yee
z	as in sizzle
zh	as in germ

Tones

The first tone is a high and level pitch indicated by the mark ‾

The second tone is a medium high and rising pitch indicated by ´

The third tone is a low, dipping pitch indicated by ˇ

The fourth tone is a high and quickly falling pitch indicated by ˋ

Terms for Crafts and Materials

jadeite	yìng yù	硬玉
nephrite	ruǎn yù	软玉
ivory (elephant)	xiàngyá	象牙
jade carving	yùshí diāokè	玉石雕刻
ivory carving	xiàngyá diāokè	象牙雕刻
wood carving	mù diāo	木雕
cloisonné	jǐngtàilán	景泰蓝
woodblock print	mùban shuǐyin	木版水印
rubbing	tàpiàn	拓片
pure silk	zhēn sī	真丝
double–sided embroidery	shuāngmiàn xìu	双面绣
carpet	dìtǎn	地毯
porcelain	cíqì	瓷器
earthenware, ceramic	táoqì	陶器
Cizhou ceramic	Cízhōu táoqì	磁州陶器
Jingdezhen porcelain	Jǐngdézhen táocì	景德镇陶器
celadon	qīngcí	青磁
eggshell porcelain	bótāi cíqì	薄胎瓷器
lacquerware	qīqì	漆器
cinnabar lacquerware	hóngqī diāoqì	红漆雕器
carved lacquerware	qídiāo	漆雕
bodiless lacquerware	tuōtāi qīqì	脱胎漆器
stencil print fabric	yìnhuā bù	印花布
batik	làrǎn	腊染
furniture	jiājù	家具
dough figure	miàn rén	面人
Tang polychrome glazed ceramic	Táng sāncǎi	唐三彩
purple sand ceramic	zǐshā táo	紫砂陶
tents	zhàngpéng	帐篷
turquoise	qīnglùsède	青绿色的

Useful Shopping Phrases

Does someone here speak English?
Yǒu méi yǒu rén huì jiǎng Yīngwén?

有没有人会讲英文？

Do you have…
Yǒu méi yǒu…

有没有

I want to buy…
Wǒ yào mǎi…

我要买

How much is this one?
Zhèige duōshǎo qían?

这个多少钱？

This is too expensive.
Zhèige tài guì.

这个太贵.

Do you have a cheaper one?
Yǒu méi yǒu piányi de?

有没有便宜的？

I would like to see that one.
Wǒ xiǎng kàn nèige.

我想看那个.

…the one below
…xiàmian de

下面的

…the one above
…shàngmian de

上面的

…the one behind
…hòumian de

后面的

Do you have a larger one?
Yǒu dà de ma?

有大的吗？

Do you have a smaller one?
Yǒu xiǎo de ma?

有小的吗？

I want to buy this one.
Wǒ yào mǎi zhèige.

我要买这个.

Do you accept credit cards?
Nǐmen shōu bù shōu xìnyòng kǎ?

你们收不收信用卡？

Do you accept travelers checks?
Nǐmen shōu bù shōu lǚxíng zhīpiào?

你们收不收旅行支票？

Please give me a receipt.
Qǐng gěi wǒ fāpiào.

请给我发票.

Is this a reproduction?
Zhèige shì fǎnggǔpǐn ma?

这个是仿古品吗？

Is this an antique?
Zhèige shì gǔdǒng ma?

这个是古董吗？

Is this carving made of nephrite or jadeite?
Zhèige diāokè shì ruǎn yù háishì yìng yù zuode?

这个雕刻是软玉还是硬玉做的？

Is this carving made of ivory from African elephants?
Zhèige diāokè shì Fēizhōu xiàngyá zuode ma?

这个雕刻是非洲象牙做的吗？

Terms Used in Store Addresses

north	běi	北
south	nán	南
east	dōng	东
west	xī	西
central	zhòng	中
road	lù, dajiē, jiē	路，大于，于
alley or lane	hútóng	胡同
intersection	kǒu	口
section	duàn	段
number	hǎo	号

Numbers and Money

cent	fēn	分
dime	máo	毛
dollar (in yuan or Y)	kuài	块
1	yī	一
2	èr	二
3	sān	三
4	sì	四
5	wǔ	五

6	liǔ	六
7	qī	七
8	bā	八
9	jiǔ	九
10	shí	十
11	shí yī	十一
12	shí èr	十二
13	shí sān	十三
20	èr shí	二十
30	sān shí	三十
100	yì bǎi	一百
101	yì bǎi yì	一百零一
1000	yì qiān	一千

| 350Y, for example, | sān bǎi wǔ shí kuài | 三百五十块钱 |

List of Friendship Stores

City	Address	Telephone
Beijing	Jianguomenwai Ave.	593514
Chengdu	519 Shengli Rd. Central	27067
Fuzhou	103 N. Bayiqi Rd.	32106
Guangzhou	369 E. Huanshi Rd.	76296
Hangzhou	302 Tiyuchang Rd.	26480
Nanjing	Zhongyang Rd.	32802
Shanghai	33 Zhongshan Rd.	219698
Suzhou	92 Guanqian St.	4972
Tianjin	2 Zhangde Ave.	32513, 33183
Wuxi	8 Chaoyang Rd.	

Index